Copyright © 2012 XXX

The right of Professor James Steinburg to be identified as the author of this work has been asserted in accordance with the Copyright, Designs and Patents Act 1988.

All rights reserved. No part of this publication may be reproduced, stored in a retrieval system, or transmitted in any form or by any means, electronic, mechanical, photocopying, recording or otherwise, without the prior permission of the publishers.

This e-Book is published by
Gold Turtle Publishing

8.3.	Day()	53
8.4.	Month()	53
8.5.	Year()	54
8.6.	Weekday()	54
8.7.	Hour()	55
8.8.	Minute()	55
8.9.	Second()	56
8.10.	Date()	56
8.11.	Time()	57
8.12.	Now()	57
9.	File and directory functions	58
9.1.	CompatabilityMode()	58
9.2.	Dir()	59
9.3.	MkDir()	59
9.4.	RmDir()	60
9.5.	FileCopy()	60
9.6.	Name	61
9.7.	Kill()	61
9.8.	FileExists()	62
9.9.	GetAttr()	62
9.10.	SetAttr()	63
9.11.	FileDateTime()	63
9.12.	FileLen()	64
9.13.	FreeFile	64
9.14.	Open	65
9.15.	Close	65
9.16.	Print	66
9.17.	Line Input	66
9.18.	Eof()	67
10.	Messages and Input Boxes	68
10.1.	MsgBox()	68
10.2.	InputBox()	70
11.	Other functions	71

11.1.	Beep	71
11.2.	Shell()	71
11.3.	Wait	72
11.4.	WaitUntil	72
11.5.	Environ()	73
12.	The OpenOfffice.org API	74
12.1.	Introduction	74
12.2.	Universal Network Objects (UNO)	74
12.3.	API Properties and methods	75
12.4.	Modules and services	75
12.5.	Identifying methods and properties	76
13.	Working with OpenOffice.org Documents	78
13.1.	The StarDesktop	78
13.2.	Document information	78
13.3.	Creating and loading documents	79
13.4.	Saving documents	80
13.5.	Printing documents	81
13.6.	Styles	82
13.7.	Templates	83
14.	Text documents (Writer)	84
14.1.	Introduction	84
14.2.	The structure of text documents	84
14.3.	Paragraphs	85
14.4.	Paragraph portions	86
14.5.	Formatting	86
14.6.	The TextCursor	88
14.7.	Non-text objects	91
14.8.	Creating a table	92
14.9.	Inserting a text frame	95
14.10.	Inserting a text field	95
14.11.	Bookmarks	97
15.	Spreadsheet Documents (Calc)	98
15.1.	Spreadsheets	98

15.2.	Rows and columns	99
15.3.	Cells and ranges	100
15.4.	Formatting cells	103
15.5.	Page properties	105
16.	Drawing documents (Draw)	110
16.1.	Document structure – pages	110
16.2.	Drawing object properties	112
16.3.	Different drawing objects	119
16.4.	Editing drawing objects	123
17.	Presentation documents (Impress)	126
17.1.	Working with presentations	126
18.	Charts	128
18.1.	Charts in spreadsheets	128
18.2.	Types of chart	128
18.3.	Chart structure	130
19.	Databases	137
19.1.	Introduction	137
19.2.	Queries	138
19.3.	Database access	139
20.	Dialogs	142
20.1.	Introduction	142
20.2.	Accessing dialogs	142
20.3.	Control element properties	144
20.4.	Dialog events	145
21.	Forms	149
21.1.	Working with form objects	149
21.2.	Control element aspects	150
21.3.	Control element types	152

1. Introduction

Apache Open Office is the leading open-source office software suite. It features word processing, spreadsheets, presentations, graphics and databases. It is available for all major operating systems.

Open Office has the ability to automate features using recorded and manually created macros, created using a number of different programming languages. This book concentrates on one of those languages OpenOffice.org Basic.

This book starts by giving an overview of the language and its structure, before detailing the various commands and functions that are available in OpenOffice.org Basic.

2. The OpenOffice.org Basic language

This chapter introduces the structure of the OpenOffice.org Basic language and gives examples of the commands that are available to the user.

2.1. The OpenOffice.org IDE

All programming in OpenOffice.org Basic is done through the IDE, which can be accessed as follows. Select -

> Tools > Macros > Organize Macros > OpenOffice.org Basic

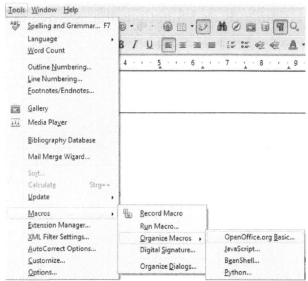

This will open up the OpenOffice.org Basic Macros dialog:

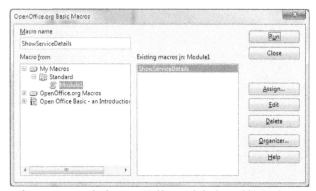

From here, you can select a module to Edit, which will bring up the IDE.

2.2. Grouping Code

OpenOffice.org Basic is based on the use of subroutines and function, which are defined using the keywords Sub and Function. The difference between a Function and a Sub is that a Function returns a value, whilst a Sub does not. Subs and Functions can call other Subs and Functions, as can be seen in the example code below -

```
Sub HelloWorld
    Dim s As String
    s = GetHelloWorldString()
    Print s
End Sub

Function GetHelloWorldString() As String
    GetHelloWorldString = "Hello World"
End Function
```

In the above example, the subroutine HelloWorld calls the function GetHelloWorldString, to obtain the text "Hello World", which is then printed.

The organisation of code within OpenOffice.org Basic can be described as the following hierarchy -

- Code is entered in a subroutine or function.
- Each subroutine or function is contained in one (and only one) module. Each module can contain 0 or more subroutines/functions.
- Each module can live in one (and only one) library. Each library can contain 0 or more modules.
- A library may be contained in 0 or more library containers and a library container can contain 1 or more libraries. A library container always contains a Standard library.
- OpenOffice.org documents are library containers, so these documents can contain libraries.

A library can be:

- Shared – as in a network install, used by multiple users.
- Just for the current user in any documents that they use.
- Stored within a document or template and only available when that document is open.

2.2.1. Optional Parameters

A parameter may be declared as optional, using the Optional keyword. The IsMissing() function can then be used to determine if the parameter was passed.

2.2.2. Parameters by reference or value

If a variable is passed by value, then if the passed parameter is changed in the called procedure then the original variable will not change. If the variable is passed by reference, then if the parameter changes so does the original variable. The default behaviour is to pass by reference.

2.2.3. Recursion

It is possible for functions to be recursive. For example, this function determines the Greatest Common Divisor of two integers

```
Function gcd(a As Integer, b As Integer) As Integer
    If b = 0 Then
        gcd = a
    Else
        gcd = gcd(b, a Mod b)
    End If
End Function
```

2.3. Comments

It is good practice to comment your code, so that other can understand it. Additionally, if you go back to some old code after a period of time, it will assist your own understanding of the code. OpenOffice.org Basic offers two ways of denoting a comment, using the single quote character (') and the Rem statement. Any text that follows is then ignored for the remainder of the line.

```
REM Here is a comment
' This is another comment
Dim s As String ' This is also a comment
```

2.4. Running the code

Basic code can be run in several ways:

- Directly from the IDE using the run button on the menu bar. This will run the first sub-routine/function in the module.
- From the tools menu – Tools > Macros > Run Macro
- By assigning the macro to a keypress.
- By assigning the macro to a menu entry.
- By assigning the macro to a toolbar button.
- By creating a control in the document
- By assigning it to an event.

2.5. Variables

2.5.1. Naming variables

Variable names can have 255 characters in them and they must start with an alphabetical character. They can contain underscores and spaces. If a name contains a space then it must be enclosed in square brackets "[]". There is no case-sensitivity in variable names, so "variable" is the same as "Variable".

2.5.2. Declaring variables

It is deemed good practice to declare your variables before you use them and this is done using the Dim statement. The syntax of Dim is as follows -

```
[Dim|ReDim] Name1 [(start To end)] [As type], Name2  [(start To end)] [As type], …
```

Using this format, it is possible to declare a number of variables at the same time. *Name1* and *Name2* are the variable names. *Start* and *end* define the number of elements in an array and can range from -32768 to 32767. Finally, *type* defines the type of variable and valid values include Boolean, Date, Double, Integer, Long, Object, String and Variant. If no type is defined then it defaults to Variant.

2.5.3. Variable scope

When a variable is declared within a Subroutine or Function, it is a local variable and is only valid for as long as the function is running. Each time the function is called, the variable is reset and the previous values are not available.

```
Sub Test()
    Dim MyInteger As Integer
End Sub
```

2.5.3.1. Static variables

If you want to have a local variable that retains its value between calls to the Function, then you have to declare it using the Static keyword.

```
Sub Test()
    Static MyInteger As Integer
End Sub
```

2.5.3.2. Public domain variables

Public domain variables are defined in the header section of a module using either the keyword Dim or the keyword Public. These variables are available to all modules in the library. A public domain variable is only available as long as the associated macro is executing and then the variable is reset.

2.5.3.3. Global variables

Global variables are similar in terms of their function to public domain variables, except that their values are retained even after the associated macro has executed. Global variable are declared in the header section of the module using the keyword Global.

2.5.3.4. Private variables

Private variables are only available in the module in which they are defined. They are declared using the Private keyword.

If several modules use a private variable with the same name, then OpenOffice.org Basic creates a different variable for each occurrence of the name.

2.5.4.   Types

OpenOffice.org Basic supports numeric, string, Boolean and object variable types. Objects are mainly used to refer to internals, such as documents and tables. With an object, you can use the objects corresponding methods and types. Numeric types are initialised to zero and strings are initialised to an empty string "".

If you need to know the variable type at runtime, then there are two functions available. TypeName() returns a string representation of the variable type, while VarType() returns an integer corresponding to the variable type.

The table below shows the values returned by TypeName() and VarType() for each type of variable

Type	TypeName()	VarType()
Boolean	Boolean	11
Currency	Currency	6
Date	Date	7
Double	Double	5
Integer	Integer	2
Long	Long	3
Object	Object	9
Single	Single Floating Point	4
String	String	S
Variant	Empty	0

2.5.4.1.   *Testing variable types*

Another way to determine the type of a variable is to use the Boolean functions IsArray, IsDate, IsEmpty, IsMissing, IsNull, IsNumeric, IsObject and IsUnoStruct.

2.5.4.2.   *Boolean variables*

Boolean variables use the values "True" and "False", which are internally represented by the values "-1" and "0" respectively. If you assign a value to a Boolean and it does not exactly evaluate to 0 then the "True" value is stored.

2.5.4.3. Integer variables

Integer variables are 16 bit numbers, with a range from -32768 to 32767. A floating point number can be assigned to an Integer, in which case it is rounded to the nearest integer value.

2.5.4.4. Long variables

Long integer variables are 32 bit number, with a range from -2,147,483,648 to 2,147,483,647. Again assigning a floating point number to a long is done by rounding to the nearest integer value.

2.5.4.5. Currency variables

Currency variables are 64 bit fixed decimal numbers, with 4 digits after the decimal point and fifteen before it. They have a range from -922,337,203,658,477.5808 to 922,337,203,658,477.5807.

2.5.4.6. Single variables

A single is a 32 bit number. The smallest magnitude is $1.401298 \times 10E\text{-}45$ and the largest magnitude is $3.402823 \times 10E38$.

2.5.4.7. Double variables

A double is a 64 bit number. The smallest magnitude is $4.94065645841247 \times 10E\text{-}324$ and the largest magnitude is $1.79769313486232 \times 10E308$.

2.5.4.8. String variables

String variables can hold character strings up to 65,535 characters in length. Each character is stored as the corresponding Unicode value.

2.5.4.9. Object, Variant, Empty and Null

When considering Object and Variant variables, to special values are of interest. The empty value indicates that no value has been assigned to the variable and the Null value indicates that no valid value is present. These values can be tested using the IsEmpty() and IsNull() functions.

When an Object is declared, it holds the value Null and when a Variant is declared, it is Empty.

A choice needs to be made as to whether to use an Object or a Variant when interacting with UNO objects. A Variant should be used to declare variables for UNO objects, and Object when declaring pure OpenOffice.org Basic objects.

2.5.5. Constants

A constant is a value that once defined doesn't change. OpenOffice.org Basic has built in Constants such as True, False and PI. You can also define your own constants using the keyword Const.

```
Const MonthsInYear = 12
```

2.5.6. Arrays

An array allows you to store many different values in a single variable. For example the String array MonthNames could be used to hold the names of the months. The first item in an array is by default stored at location 0. However, you can specify the starting and ending values. For example

```
Dim i(5) As Double ' 6 elements from 0 to 5 inclusive
Dim s(5 to 10) As String ' 6 elements from 5 to 10 inclusive
```

If you want to fill an array with data quickly, then you can use the Array() function. This returns a Variant array with the included data. For example

```
Sub ArrayPopulation()
    Dim DaysOfWeek()
    DaysOfWeek = Array("Monday", "Tuesday", "Wednesday", "Thursday", "Friday", _
        "Saturday", "Sunday")
End Sub
```

2.5.6.1. Option Base

If you want to change the default lower bound of all arrays to start from 1 rather than 0, then this must be done before any other executable statement in the program, in the following format

```
Option Base { 0 | 1 }
```

2.5.6.2. LBound and UBound

The LBound and UBound functions return the lower and upper bounds of an array. The format of the functions is LBound(ArrayName, [Dimension]) and UBound(ArrayName, [Dimension]). The optional second parameter is used for multi-dimensional arrays and specifies the position of the index for which you want to know the upper/lower values.

1. Introduction 1

2. The OpenOffice.org Basic language 2

   2.1. The OpenOffice.org IDE 2

   2.2. Grouping Code 3

   2.3. Comments 4

   2.4. Running the code 5

   2.5. Variables 5

   2.6. Comparison operators 10

   2.7. Logical operators 11

   2.8. Branching and Looping 11

   2.9. Error handling 16

   2.10. Other instructions 17

   2.11. Operators and Precedence 19

   2.12. String manipulations 20

   2.13. Numeric manipulations 22

   2.14. Date manipulations 23

   2.15. File manipulations 24

3. Mathematical operators 26

   3.1. Addition operator (+) 26

   3.2. Subtraction operator (-) 26

   3.3. Multiplication operator (*) 27

   3.4. Division operator (/) 27

   3.5. Rounded Division operator (\) 28

   3.6. Power operator (^) 28

   3.7. String concatenation operator (&) 29

   3.8. MOD operator 29

4. Logical operators 30

   4.1. AND operator 30

   4.2. EQV operator 31

   4.3. IMP operator 32

   4.4. NOT operator 33

   4.5. OR operator 34

4.6.	XOR operator	35
5.	Comparison operators	36
5.1.	Equality operator (=)	36
5.2.	Inequality operator (<>)	37
5.3.	Greater than operator (>)	37
5.4.	Greater than or equal to operator (>=)	38
5.5.	Less than operator (<)	39
5.6.	Less than or equal to operator (<=)	39
6.	Conversion Functions	40
6.1.	Implicit type conversions	40
6.2.	CStr()	41
6.3.	CInt()	41
6.4.	CLng()	42
6.5.	CSng()	42
6.6.	CDbl()	43
6.7.	CBool()	43
6.8.	CDate()	44
6.9.	Val()	44
6.10.	IsNumeric()	45
6.11.	IsDate()	45
6.12.	IsArray()	46
7.	String functions	47
7.1.	Asc()	47
7.2.	Chr()	47
7.3.	Left()	48
7.4.	Right()	48
7.5.	Mid()	49
7.6.	Len()	50
7.7.	InStr()	50
7.8.	Format()	51
8.	Date and time functions	52
8.1.	DateSerial()	52
8.2.	TimeSerial()	52

2.5.6.3. *DimArray*

The DimArray() function is used to set or change the number of dimensions in a Variant array.

2.5.6.4. *ReDim*

The ReDim function is used to change the number of elements in an array. For example

```
Sub ReDimming()
    Dim a(10) ' 0 to 10 are valid
    ReDim a(20) ' 0 to 20 are now valid
End Sub
```

If you wish to preserve the contents of an array when it is re-dimensioned, then you need to use the Preserve keyword.

2.6. Comparison operators

There are a number of operators that are available for providing comparisons of variables. These are summarised below

Symbol	Description
=	Equal to
<	Less than
>	Greater than
<=	Less than or equal to
>=	Greater than or equal to
<>	Not equal to
Is	Are these the same Object

2.7. Logical operators

There are also logical operators which operate on comparing Boolean types

Symbol	Description
AND	Both variables are True
OR	One or both variables is True
XOR	Only one of the variables is True
NOT	Negates a single Boolean variable

2.8. Branching and Looping

2.8.1. If Then Else

The If construct is used to execute a block of code based on the results of an expression. The syntax of the If construct is as follows

```
If condition = True Then
    StatementBlock
[ElseIf condition = True Then]
    StatementBlock
[Else]
    StatementBlock
End If
```

For example

```
If i < 0 Then
    Print "The number is negative"
ElseIf i > 0 Then
    Print "The number is positive"
Else
    Print "The number is 0"
End If
```

2.8.2. IIF

The IIF construct returns an expression based on a condition. The syntax is

```
IIF(Condition, TrueExpression, FalseExpression)
```

It is a more compact way of writing the following If construct

```
If (Condition) Then
    a = TrueExpression
Else
    a = FalseExpression
End If
```

An example of the IIF construct is

```
YoungestAge = IIF(HarryAge < JohnAge, HarryAge, JohnAge)
```

2.8.3.   Choose

The Choose statement allows you to choose from a list of values based on an index. The syntax of Choose is

```
Choose(Index, Selection1[, Selection2, ..., SelectionN])
```

If the index is 1 then the first item is returned, and so on. For example

```
DayValue = 5
Choose(DayValue, "Monday", "Tuesday", "Wednesday", "Thursday", "Friday", "Saturday", "Sunday")
```

would return "Friday".

2.8.4.   For ... Next

The For...Next construct runs a block of code a specified number of times. The syntax is

```
For Counter = Start To End [Step step]
    StatementBlock
    [Exit For]
Next [Counter]
```

The numeric counter is initially assigned the "start" value and if a step value is not given, it is incremented by 1 until it passes the "end" value. If a step value is given then the "step" is added to the counter. The statement block is executed once for each increment. It is possible for the step value to be negative, in which case the loop counts down from Start to End and Start must be greater than End.

The "counter" after the Next statement is optional, and if it is not specified then it automatically refers to the most recent For statement.

If you wish to leave a For loop prematurely, then you can use the "Exit For" statement, which will leave the most recent For loop.

For example

```
Sub ArrayPopulation()
    Dim DaysOfWeek()
    Dim DayNumber As Integer
    DaysOfWeek = Array("Monday", "Tuesday", "Wednesday", "Thursday", "Friday", _
        "Saturday", "Sunday")
    For DayNumber = LBound(DaysOfWeek()) To UBound(DaysOfWeek())
        Print DaysOfWeek(DayNumber)
    Next
End Sub
```

2.8.5.   Do Loop

The Do Loop has a number of distinct forms and is used to execute a block of code while a condition is True. The most common form checks the condition before the loop is run and as long as the condition is true will repeatedly execute the statement block. If the condition is initially false, then the loop will never execute

```
Do While Condition
    StatementBlock
Loop
```

A less common form checks the condition before the loop starts and executes the statement block until the condition is true. If the condition is initially true then the loop will never execute

```
Do Until Condition
    StatementBlock
Loop
```

It is also possible to place the check at the end of the loop, in which case the code will always be executed at least once

```
Do
    StatementBlock
Loop While Condition
```

To always execute the loop at least once, and then continue as long as the condition is false use the following construct

```
Do
    StatementBlock
Loop Until Condition
```

It is possible to force an immediate exit from the loop using the "Exit Do" statement.

2.8.6. Select Case

The Select Case statement mimics multiple "Else If" blocks in an "If" statement. A single condition is specified, which is compared against multiple values for a match. The syntax is as follows

```
Select Case Condition
    Case expression_value1
        StatementBlock
    Case expression_value2
        StatementBlock
    Case Else
        StatementBlock
End Select
```

The first statement block to match the condition is executed and if none match then the optional Case Else will match.

2.8.6.1. *Case expressions*

A case expression is usually a constant, such as "5" or "First". Multiple values may be specified by separating them with commas. It is also possible to check a range of values using a "To" keyword ("Case 3 To 6") and open-ended ranges can be checked, such as "Case > 5".

2.8.7. While ... Wend

The While ... Wend construct just executes a statement block while the condition is true. The syntax is

```
While Condition
    StatementBlock
Wend
```

2.8.8. GoSub

The GoSub statement causes execution to jump to a defined label in the current procedure. The code will execute at the new location, until it reached a Return statement, when it will continue from the point of the original call. An example of a GoSub is

```
Sub GoSubExample()
    Dim i As Integer
    i = 1
    GoSub Line1
    Print "i = " + i
    Exit Sub
Line1:
    i = 5
    Return
End Sub
```

It is not desirable to use GoSubs, as they tend to lead to code that is difficult to read and follow.

2.8.9. GoTo

The GoTo statement causes execution to jump to a defined label in the current subroutine. For example

```
Sub GoToExample()
    Dim i As Integer
    i = 10
    GoTo TheEnd
    ' This section of code will never be run
    i = i * 2
TheEnd:
    Print "i = " + i
End Sub
```

As with GoSubs, GoTo is discouraged, due to the complexities that it brings to code.

2.8.10. On GoTo and On GoSub

These two constructs are used to GoSub or GoTo based on a numeric expression, which can be between 0 and 255. The syntax of the two statements is

```
On N GoSub Label1, [Label2, Label3, ...]
On N GoTo Label1, [Label2, Label3, ...]
```

2.8.11. Exit

The Exit statement is used to exit a Do Loop, For Next, Function or Sub. The syntaxes are as follows

- Exit Do – immediately exit a Do Loop
- Exit For – immediately exit a For Loop
- Exit Function – immediately exit the current function
- Exit Sub – immediately exit the current Sub

2.9. Error handling

2.9.1. On Error

There are a number of types of error that can be encountered whilst your macro is running, some can be checked for and handled accordingly, such as missing files. Others you need to trap. Errors are trapped using the "On Error" statement

```
On [Local] Error { GoTo Label | GoTo 0 | Resume Next }
```

On Error allows you to specify the action to be taken in handling an error, including setting up your own error handler. If "Local" is used then this defines an error handling routine local to the Sub or Function. If "Local" is not used then the error handling affects the entire module.

2.9.1.1. Specifying how to handle an error

To ignore all errors use "On Error Resume Next". When this is used, the statement that caused the error will be skipped and the next statement executed.

If you want to set up your own error handler then use "On Error GoTo Label". When an error occurs, execution will be transferred to the label.

You can also use "On Error GoTo 0" to specify that the default method of handling an error should be used (stopping the macro execution with an error message).

2.9.1.2. *Writing your error handler*

There are a number of functions that will help you to determine what happened and where it happened.

- Err() returns the error number of the last error.
- Error([Num]) returns the error message as a string. If the optional numeric parameter Num is used then Error will return the error message for that error number.
- Erl() returns the line number where the last error occurred.
- After the error has been handled, you must decide how to proceed.
- Do nothing and allow execution to continue.
- Exit the Sub or Function using "Exit Sub" or "Exit Function".
- Use "Resume" to execute the same line again.
- Use "Resume Next" to execute the line immediately after the one the error occurred on.
- Use "Resume Label:" to continue execution at a specified label.

2.10. Other instructions

2.10.1. Type ... End Type

2.10.1.1. *Definition*

A *struct* is a collection of data fields that can be manipulated as a single item. Using the Type ... End Type statements, you can define your own structs:

```
Type aMenuItem 'assign the name of the type
    'Define the data fields within the struct. Each
    ' definition looks like a Dim statement, without the "Dim".
    aCommand As String
    aText As String
End Type 'close the definition
```

2.10.1.2. *Instance*

The Type definition is just a template, not an actual variable. To make an instance of the struct you have to use the Dim As New statement

```
Dim mItem As New aMenuItem
```

2.10.1.3. *Accessing the data*

Basic does not in general look inside a container to see what names are defined there. If you want to use such a name, you must tell Basic where to look. This is done by using the container name as a *qualifier*, followed by a period

```
myCommand = mItem.aCommand
```

As containers may hold other containers, you may need more than one qualifier. They should be written in order from outer to inner, separated by periods.

2.10.2. With … End With

The With … End With statements provide an alternative to writing out all the qualifiers. You specify the qualifiers in the With statement and until Basic encounters an End With statement, it looks for partly-qualified names (beginning with a period)

```
Type aMenuItem
    aCommand As String
    aText As String
End Type

Sub Main()
    ' Create an instance of the user-defined struct
    Dim mItem As New aMenuItem
    With mItem
        .aCommand = ".uno:Copy"
        .aText = "~Copy"
    End With
End Sub
```

2.11. Operators and Precedence

OpenOffice.org Basic supports the standard numerical operators -, +, /, * and ^. The operators are used in the normal precedence order. The full list of operators and their precedence are

Precedence	Operator	Description
0	AND	Bitwise on numerics and logical on Booleans
0	OR	Bitwise on numerics and logical on Booleans
0	XOR	Bitwise on numerics and logical on Booleans
0	EQV	Logical and/or bitwise equivalence
0	IMP	Logical Implication
1	=	Logical
1	<	Logical
1	>	Logical
1	<=	Logical
1	>=	Logical
1	<>	Logical
2	-	Numeric subtraction
2	+	Numeric addition and string concatenation
3	&	String Concatenation
3	*	Numeric multiplication
3	/	Numeric division
3	MOD	Numeric remainder after division
4	^	Numeric Exponentiation

2.12. String manipulations

There are a number of functions that are available for the manipulation of strings, as shown below

Function	Description
Asc(s$)	ASCII value of the first character in the string.
Chr$(i)	Return the character corresponding to the ASCII code.
Format(number[, f])	Format the number based on the format string.
Hex(number)	String that represents the hexadecimal value of a number.
InStr([i,] s$, f$[, c])	Position of f in s, 0 if not found. The return type is a Long value coerced into an Integer, so it can be negative for large strings.
LCase(s$)	Returns the string all in lower case.
Left(s$, n)	Returns the leftmost n characters from s.
Len(s$)	Returns the length of string s.
LSet s$ = Text	Left align a string.
LTrim(s$)	Return the string s with no leading spaces.
Mid(s$, i[, n])	Substring from location i for n characters.
Mid(s$, i, n, r$)	Replace the substring with the contents of r.
Oct(number)	String representing the Octal value of a number.
Right(s$, n)	Return the rightmost n characters from s.
RSet s$ = Text	Right align a string
Space(n)	Returns a string that consists of n spaces.
Str(Expression)	Convers the numeric expression into a string.
StrComp(x$, y$[, c])	Returns -1 if x > y, 0 if x = y, and 1 if x < y. If c = 1 then case-insensitive.
String(n, {i | s$})	Create a string with n characters. If an integer is used, this is considered the ASCII character to repeat. If a string is used then the first character is repeated n times.
Trim(s$)	Returns a string with no leading or trailing spaces.
UCase(s$)	Returns the string as all upper case.
Val(s$)	Converts the string to a number.

2.12.1. Removing characters from a string

The following Function will remove characters from a string.

```
'Remove a certain number of characters from a string
Function RemoveFromString(s$, index&, num&) As String
    If num = 0 Or Len(s) < index Then
        'If removing nothing or outside the range then return the string
        RemoveFromString = s
    ElseIf index <= 1 Then
        'Removing from the start
        If num >= Len(s) Then
            RemoveFromString = ""
        Else
            RemoveFromString = Right(s, Len(s) - num)
        End If
    Else
        'Removing from the middle
        If index + num > Len(s) Then
            RemoveFromString = Left(s, index - 1)
        Else
            RemoveFromString = Left(s, index - 1) + Right(s, Len(s) - index - num + 1)
        End If
    End If
End Function
```

2.12.2. Replace text in a string

The following function will replace a portion of a string with new text.

```
Function ReplaceInString(s$, index&, num&, replaces$) As String
    If index <= 1 Then
        'Place this in front of the string
        If num < 1 Then
            ReplaceInString = replaces + s
        ElseIf num > Len(s) Then
            ReplaceInString = replaces
        Else
            ReplaceInString = replaces + Right(s, Len(s) - num)
        End If
    ElseIf index + num > Len(s) Then
        ReplaceInString = Left(s, index - 1) + replaces
    Else
        ReplaceInString = Left(s, index - 1) + replaces + Right(s, Len(s) - index - num + 1)
    End If
End Function
```

2.12.3. Remove all occurrences of a String

This macro will delete all occurrences of the String bad from s

```
Sub RemoveFromString(s$, bad$)
    Dim i%
    i = InStr(s, bad)
    Do While i > 0
        Mid(s, i, Len(bad), "")
        i = InStr(i, s, bad)
    Loop
End Sub
```

2.13. Numeric manipulations

OpenOffice.org Basic also provides a number of functions for the manipulation of numeric variables

Function	Description
Abs(Number)	Returns the absolute value of a number as a Double.
Atn(x)	Returns the angle, in radians, whose tangent is x.
Blue(colour)	Returns the Blue component of a given colour code.
CByte(Expression)	Convert a string or number to a byte.
CDbl(Expression)	Convert a string or number to a Double.
CInt(Expression)	Convert a string or number to a Integer.
CLng(Expression)	Convert a string or number to a Long.
Cos(x)	Calculates the cosine of an angle specified in radians.
CSng(Expression)	Convert a string or number to a single precision number.
CStr(Expression)	Convert the numeric expression to a string.
Exp(Expression)	Base of the natural logarithm (e = 2.718282) raised to a power.
Fix(Expression)	Return the integer portion of a number.
Green(colour)	Returns the Green component of a colour code.
Int(Number)	Rounds the integer towards infinity.
Randomize [Number]	Initialises the random number generator.
Red(colour)	Returns the Red component of a colour code.
RGB(Red, Green, Blue)	Long colour value consisting of Red, Green and Blue components.
Rnd [(Expression)]	Returns a random number between 0 and 1.
Sgn(Number)	Returns 1, -1 or 0 if the number is positive, negative or zero.

Sin(x)	Calculates the sine of an angle specified in radians.
Sqr(Number)	Square root of a numeric expression.
Tan(x)	Calculates the tangent of an angle specified in radians.

2.14. Date manipulations

There are also a number of functions for the manipulation of dates.

Function	Description
CDate(Expression)	Converts a string or number to a date.
CDateFromIso(String)	Returns the internal date number from a string containing a date in ISO format.
CDateToIso(Number)	Returns the date in ISO format from a serial date number that was generated with DateSerial or DateValue.
Date	Returns the current system date.
Date = s$	Sets the current system date.
DateSerial(y%, m%, d%)	Return a date from the year, month and day.
DateValue([date])	Returns a Long from a date.
Day(Number)	Returns the day of the month number from a date generated by DateSerial or DateValue.
GetSystemTicks()	Returns the system ticks provided by the operating system.
Hour(Number)	Returns the hour from a time generated by TimeSerial or TimeValue.
Minute(Number)	Returns the minutes from a time generated by TimeSerial or TimeValue.
Month(Number)	Returns the month from a date generated by DateSerial or DateValue.
Now	Current system time and date as a Date value.
Second(Number)	Returns the seconds from a time generated by TimeSerial or TimeValue.
Time	Current system time.
Timer	Number of seconds that have elapsed since midnight.
TimeSerial(h%, m%, s%)	Serial time value from the specified hour, minute and second.
TimeValue(s$)	Serial time value from a formatted string.
Wait millisec	Pause for a given number of milliseconds.

| WeekDay(Number) | Returns the day of the week from a date generated by DateSerial or DateValue. |
| Year(Number) | Returns the year from a date generated by DateSerial or DateValue. |

2.15. File manipulations

A number of functions are also provided for interacting with the file system.

Function	Description
Close #n% [,n2%[,...]]	Closes files opened with an Open statement.
ConvertFromURL(s$)	Converts a file URL to a system file name.
ConvertToURL(s$)	Converts a system file name to a file URL.
CurDir([s$])	Returns the current directory of the specified drive.
Dir [s$ [, Attrib%]]	Perform a directory listing.
EOF(n%)	Has the file pointer reached the end of the file?
FileAttr(n%, Attribut%)	Return the file attribute of an open file.
FileCopy from$, to$	Copy a file.
FileDateTime(s$)	Returns a string of the file date and time.
FileExists(s$)	Determines whether a file or directory exists.
FileLen(s$)	The length of the file in bytes.
FreeFile	The next available file number.
Get [#]n%, [Pos], v	Read a record or bytes from a file.
GetAttr(s$)	Returns a bit pattern that identifies the file type.
Input #n%, v1[, v2 [,...]]	Read data from an open sequential file.
Kill f$	Delete a file from disk.
Line Input #%, v$	Read a string from a sequential file into a variable.
Loc(n%)	Returns the current position in an open file.
Lof(n%)	Returns the current size of an open file.
MkDir s$	Creates a new directory.
Name old$, new$	Renames an existing file or directory.

Open s$ [#]n%	Open a file for reading or writing.
Pun [#]n%, [Pos], v	Writes a record or sequence of bytes to a file.
Reset	Closes all open files and flushes all buffers to disk.
RmDir f$	Removes a directory.
Seek [#]n%, Pos	Moves the file pointer.
SetAttr f$, Attribute%	Sets the file attributes.
Write [#]n%, [Exprs]	Write data to a sequential file.

3. Mathematical operators

We will now summarise all of the operators that are available in OpenOffice.org Basic, together with their syntax and an example of their use.

3.1. Addition operator (+)

Adds two numerical values. The addition operator can also be used for the concatenation of strings.

3.1.1. Syntax

```
Result = Expression1 + Expression2
```

3.1.2. Parameters

Result: The result of the addition.

Expression1, Expression2: Any numerical expression.

3.1.3. Example

```
Sub AdditionExample()
    Print 15 + 4 ' Prints 19
End Sub

Sub AdditionExample2()
    Print "Hello" + "World" ' Prints "Hello World"
End Sub
```

3.2. Subtraction operator (-)

Subtracts two numerical values.

3.2.1. Syntax

```
Result = Expression1 – Expression2
```

3.2.2. Parameters

Result: The result of the subtraction.

Expression1, Expression2: Any numerical expression.

3.2.3. Example

```
Sub SubtractionExample()
    Print 10 – 3 ' Prints 7
End Sub
```

3.3. Multiplication operator (*)

Multiplies two numerical values.

3.3.1. Syntax

```
Result = Expression1 *Expression2
```

3.3.2. Parameters

Result: The result of the multiplication.

Expression1, Expression2: Any numerical expression.

3.3.3. Example

```
Sub MultiplicationExample()
    Print 5 * 5 ' Prints 25
End Sub
```

3.4. Division operator (/)

Divides two numerical values. You need to be careful when using this function as due to the way numbers are stored, the number might not be exactly the value you expect it to be. For example, the number 1 might be stored as 1.0000001, which will give a discrepancy in the result. If accuracy is important use the Int() function.

3.4.1. Syntax

```
Result = Expression1 / Expression2
```

3.4.2. Parameters

Result: The result of the division.

Expression1, Expression2: Any numerical expression.

3.4.3. Example

```
Sub DivisionExample()
    Print 15 / 5 ' Prints 3
End Sub
```

3.5. Rounded Division operator (\)

Divides two numerical values with a whole number result.

3.5.1. Syntax

```
Result = Expression1 \ Expression2
```

3.5.2. Parameters

Result: The result of the division.

Expression1, Expression2: Any numerical expression.

3.5.3. Example

```
Sub RoundedDivisionExample()
    Print 16 / 5 ' Prints 3.2
    Print 16 \ 5 ' Prints 3
End Sub
```

3.6. Power operator (^)

Raises a number to a power. Equivalent to the formula $x = y^z$.

3.6.1. Syntax

```
Result = Expression ^ Exponent
```

3.6.2. Parameters

Result: The result of the addition.

Expression, Exponent: Any numerical expression.

3.6.3. Example

```
Sub ExponentiationExample()
    Print 2 ^ 2 ' Prints 4
End Sub
```

3.7. String concatenation operator (&)

Concatenates two strings together in the same way that the + operator does.

3.7.1. Syntax

```
Result = String1 & String2
```

3.7.2. Parameters

Result: The result of the concatenation.

String1, String2: Any string values.

3.7.3. Example

```
Sub ConcatinationExample()
    Print "Hello " & "World" ' Prints "Hello World"
End Sub
```

3.8. MOD operator

Calculates the remainder of a division.

3.8.1. Syntax

```
Result = Expression1 MOD Expression2
```

3.8.2. Parameters

Result: The remainder result of the division.

Expression1, Expression2: Any numerical values.

3.8.3. Example

```
Sub ModExample()
    Print 15 MOD 6 ' Prints 3
End Sub
```

4. Logical operators

4.1. AND operator

Performs a logical AND on Boolean values and a bitwise AND on numerical values. The results of this operation are summarised in the table below

x	y	x AND y
TRUE	TRUE	TRUE
TRUE	FALSE	FALSE
FALSE	TRUE	FALSE
FALSE	FALSE	FALSE
1	1	1
1	0	0
0	1	0
0	0	0

4.1.1. Syntax

```
Result = Expression1 AND Expression2
```

4.1.2. Parameters

Result: The result of the operation.

Expression1, Expression2: Any numerical or Boolean expression.

4.1.3. Example

```
Sub AndExample()
    Print (5 AND 1) ' Prints 1
    Print (True AND True) ' Prints -1
    Print (True AND False) ' Prints 0
End Sub
```

4.2. EQV operator

Calculates the logic equivalence of two expressions. In a bit-wise comparison, the EQV operator sets the corresponding bin in the result only if a bit is set in both expressions, or neither expression. The results of this operation are summarised in the table below

x	y	x EQV y
TRUE	TRUE	TRUE
TRUE	FALSE	FALSE
FALSE	TRUE	FALSE
FALSE	FALSE	TRUE
1	1	1
1	0	0
0	1	0
0	0	1

4.2.1. Syntax

```
Result = Expression1 EQV Expression2
```

4.2.2. Parameters

Result: The result of the operation.

Expression1, Expression2: Any numerical or Boolean expression.

4.2.3. Example

```
Sub ExampleEQV()
    Dim vA as Variant, vB as Variant, vC as Variant, vD as Variant
    Dim vOut as Variant
    vA = 10: vB = 8: vC = 6: vD = Null
    vOut = vA > vB EQV vB > vC REM returns -1
    Print vOut
    vOut = vB > vA EQV vB > vC REM returns 0
    Print vOut
    vOut = vA > vB EQV vB > vD REM returns 0
    Print vOut
    vOut = (vB > vD EQV vB > vA) REM returns -1
    Print vOut
    vOut = vB EQV vA REM returns -3
    Print vOut
End Sub
```

4.3. IMP operator

Performs a logical implication on two expressions. If you use the IMP operator on Boolean expressions then False is only returned if first expression evaluates to True and the second expression to False. If IMP is used on a bit expression then a bit is deleted from the result if the corresponding bit is set in the first expression and the corresponding bit is not set in the second expression The results of this operation are summarised in the table below

x	y	x IMP y
TRUE	TRUE	TRUE
TRUE	FALSE	FALSE
FALSE	TRUE	TRUE
FALSE	FALSE	TRUE
1	1	1
1	0	0
0	1	1
0	0	1

4.3.1. Syntax

```
Result = Expression1 IMP Expression2
```

4.3.2. Parameters

Result: The result of the operation.

Expression1, Expression2: Any numerical or Boolean expression.

4.3.3. Example

```
Sub ExampleIMP()
    Dim vA as Variant, vB as Variant, vC as Variant, vD as Variant
    Dim vOut as Variant
    vA = 10: vB = 8: vC = 6: vD = Null
    vOut = vA > vB IMP vB > vC REM returns -1
    Print vOut
    vOut = vB > vA IMP vB > vC REM returns -1
    Print vOut
    vOut = vA > vB IMP vB > vD REM returns 0
    Print vOut
    vOut = (vB > vD IMP vB > vA) REM returns -1
    Print vOut
End Sub
```

4.4. NOT operator

Performs a logical implication on two expressions. If you use the IMP operator on Boolean expressions then False is only returned if first expression evaluates to True and the second expression to False. If IMP is used on a bit expression then a bit is deleted from the result if the corresponding bit is set in the first expression and the corresponding bit is not set in the second expression The results of this operation are summarised in the table below

x	NOT x
TRUE	FALSE
FALSE	TRUE
1	1
0	1

4.4.1. Syntax

Result = NOT Expression

4.4.2. Parameters

Result: The result of the operation.

Expression: Any numerical or Boolean expression.

4.4.3. Example

```
Sub ExampleNOT()
    Dim vA as Variant, vB as Variant, vC as Variant, vD as Variant
    Dim vOut as Variant
    vA = True: vB = False: vC = 1: vD = 0
    vOut = NOT vA REM returns 0
    Print vOut
    vOut = NOT vB REM returns -1
    Print vOut
    vOut = NOT vC REM returns -2
    Print vOut
    vOut = NOT vD REM returns -1
    Print vOut
End Sub
```

4.5. OR operator

Performs a logical OR on Boolean values and a bitwise OR on numerical values. The results of this operation are summarised in the table below

x	y	x OR y
TRUE	TRUE	TRUE
TRUE	FALSE	TRUE
FALSE	TRUE	TRUE
FALSE	FALSE	FALSE
1	1	1
1	0	1
0	1	1
0	0	0

4.5.1. Syntax

```
Result = Expression1 OR Expression2
```

4.5.2. Parameters

Result: The result of the operation.

Expression1, Expression2: Any numerical or Boolean expression.

4.5.3. Example

```
Sub OrExample()
    Print (5 OR 1) ' Prints 5
    Print (True OR True) ' Prints -1
    Print (True OR False) ' Prints -1
    Print (False OR True) ' Prints -1
    Print (False OR False) ' Prints 0
End Sub
```

4.6. XOR operator

Performs a logical XOR on Boolean values and a bitwise XOR on numerical values. The results of this operation are summarised in the table below

x	y	x XOR y
TRUE	TRUE	FALSE
TRUE	FALSE	TRUE
FALSE	TRUE	TRUE
FALSE	FALSE	FALSE
1	1	0
1	0	1
0	1	1
0	0	0

4.6.1. Syntax

```
Result = Expression1 OR Expression2
```

4.6.2. Parameters

Result: The result of the operation.

Expression1, Expression2: Any numerical or Boolean expression.

4.6.3. Example

```
Sub XOrExample()
    Print (5 XOR 1) ' Prints 4
    Print (True XOR True) ' Prints 0
    Print (True XOR False) ' Prints -1
    Print (False XOR True) ' Prints -1
    Print (False XOR False) ' Prints 0
End Sub
```

5. Comparison operators

Comparison operators can be applied to all of the elementary variable types (numbers, dates, strings and Boolean values). Comparison operators are commonly used in If statements. All of the comparison operators return a true or a false.

5.1. Equality operator (=)

Compares whether the two expressions are equal. The equal sign is also used for assigning a value to a variable.

5.1.1. Syntax

```
Expression1 = Expression2
variable = value
```

5.1.2. Parameters

Expression1, Expression2: Any elementary variables.

5.1.3. Example

```
Sub EqualityExample()
    Dim iA As Integer, iB As Integer, iC As Integer
    iA = 5: iB = 10: iC = 5
    If iA = iB Then
        Print "This line of code is never executed"
    End If
    If iA = iC Then
        Print "This line of code is executed"
    End If
End Sub
```

5.2. Inequality operator (<>)

Compares whether the two expressions are not equal.

5.2.1. Syntax

```
Expression1 <> Expression2
```

5.2.2. Parameters

Expression1, Expression2: Any elementary variables.

5.2.3. Example

```
Sub EqualityExample()
    Dim iA As Integer, iB As Integer, iC As Integer
    iA = 5: iB = 10: iC = 5
    If iA <> iB Then
        Print "This line of code is executed"
    End If
    If iA <> iC Then
        Print "This line of code is never executed"
            End If
End Sub
```

5.3. Greater than operator (>)

Compares whether expression1 is greater than expression2.

5.3.1. Syntax

```
Expression1 > Expression2
```

5.3.2. Parameters

Expression1, Expression2: Any elementary variables.

5.3.3. Example

```
Sub GreaterThanExample()
    Dim iA As Integer, iB As Integer
    iA = 10: iB = 5
    If iA > iB Then
        Print "This line of code is executed"
    End If
    If iB > iA Then
        Print "This line of code is never executed"
    End If
End Sub
```

5.4. Greater than or equal to operator (>=)

Compares whether expression1 is greater than or equal to expression2.

5.4.1. Syntax

Expression1 >= Expression2

5.4.2. Parameters

Expression1, Expression2: Any elementary variables.

5.4.3. Example

```
Sub GreaterThanOrEqualToExample()
    Dim iA As Integer, iB As Integer, iC As Integer
    iA = 10: iB = 5: iC = 5
    If iA >= iB Then
        Print "This line of code is executed"
    End If
    If iB >= iA Then
        Print "This line of code is never executed"
    End If
    If iB >= iC Then
        Print "This line of code is executed"
    End If
End Sub
```

5.5. Less than operator (<)

Compares whether expression1 is less than expression2.

5.5.1. Syntax

```
Expression1 > Expression2
```

5.5.2. Parameters

Expression1, Expression2: Any elementary variables.

5.5.3. Example

```
Sub LessThanExample()
    Dim iA As Integer, iB As Integer
    iA = 10: iB = 5
    If iA < iB Then
        Print "This line of code is never executed"
    End If
    If iB < iA Then
        Print "This line of code is executed"
    End If
End Sub
```

5.6. Less than or equal to operator (<=)

Compares whether expression1 is less than or equal to expression2.

5.6.1. Syntax

```
Expression1 <= Expression2
```

5.6.2. Parameters

Expression1, Expression2: Any elementary variables.

5.6.3. Example

```
Sub LessThanOrEqualToExample()
    Dim iA As Integer, iB As Integer, iC As Integer
    iA = 10: iB = 5: iC = 5
    If iA <= iB Then
        Print "This line of code is never executed"
    End If
    If iB <= iA Then
        Print "This line of code is executed"
    End If
    If iB <= iC Then
        Print "This line of code is executed"
    End If
End Sub
```

6. Conversion Functions

There are often circumstances when a variable of one type needs to be changed to a variable of another type. OpenOffice.org Basic provides a number of means and functions for performing this conversion.

6.1. Implicit type conversions

The simplest way of converting a variable from one type to another is to use an assignment.

```
Dim A As String, B As Integer

B = 101
A = B
```

In this example, variable B is automatically converted to a String during the assignment to variable A. There are however pitfalls to relying on implicit conversions. Consider the following example

```
Dim A As String, B As Integer, C As Integer

B = 1
C = 1
A = B + C
```

At first glance, this seems straightforward. The Basic interpreter first calculates the result of the addition and then converts this to a string, giving the result of "2".

However, if the Basic interpreter had first converted the values of A and B to strings and then applied the + Operator, then the result would have been "11".

To avoid errors of implicit type conversions, Basic offers a number of conversion which you can use to explicitly convert the variable type.

6.2. CStr()

Converts any data type into a String.

6.2.1. Syntax

```
String = CStr(Variable)
```

6.2.2. Parameters

String: The resulting string variable.

Variable: Any non-String variable

6.2.3. Example

```
Sub CStrExample()
    Dim iA As Integer, iB As Integer, sC As String
    iA = 1: iB = 1
    sC = CStr(iA + iB)
    Print sC ' Prints "2"
    sC = CStr(iA) + CStr(iB)
    Print sC ' Prints "11"
End Sub
```

6.3. CInt()

Converts any data type into a Integer.

6.3.1. Syntax

```
Integer = CInt(Variable)
```

6.3.2. Parameters

Integer: The resulting integer variable.

Variable: Any non-integer variable

6.3.3. Example

```
Sub CIntExample()
    Dim sA As String, sB As String, iC As Integer
    sA = "1": sB = "1"
    iC = CInt(sA + sB)
    Print iC ' Prints "11"
    iC = CInt(sA) + CInt(sB)
    Print iC ' Prints "2"
End Sub
```

6.4. CLng()

Converts any data type into a Long.

6.4.1. Syntax

```
Long = CLng(Variable)
```

6.4.2. Parameters

Long: The resulting long variable.

Variable: Any non-long variable

6.4.3. Example

```
Sub CLngExample()
    Dim sA As String, sB As String, iC As Long
    sA = "1": sB = "1"
    iC = CLng(sA + sB)
    Print iC ' Prints "11"
    iC = CLng(sA) + CLng(sB)
    Print iC ' Prints "2"
End Sub
```

6.5. CSng()

Converts any data type into a Single value.

6.5.1. Syntax

```
Single = CSng(Variable)
```

6.5.2. Parameters

Single: The resulting single variable.

Variable: Any non-single variable

6.5.3. Example

```
Sub CSngExample()
    Dim sA As String, sB As String, iC As Single
    sA = "1.5": sB = "1"
    iC = CSng(sA + sB)
    Print iC ' Prints "1.51"
    iC = CSng(sA) + CSng(sB)
    Print iC ' Prints "2.5"
End Sub
```

6.6. CDbl()

Converts any data type into a Double value.

6.6.1. Syntax

```
Double = CDbl(Variable)
```

6.6.2. Parameters

Double: The resulting double variable.

Variable: Any non-double variable

6.6.3. Example

```
Sub CDblExample()
    Dim sA As String, sB As String, iC As Double
    sA = "1.5": sB = "1"
    iC = CDbl(sA + sB)
    Print iC ' Prints "1.51"
    iC = CDbl(sA) + CDbl(sB)
    Print iC ' Prints "2.5"
End Sub
```

6.7. CBool()

Converts any data type into a Boolean value.

6.7.1. Syntax

```
Boolean = CBool(Variable)
```

6.7.2. Parameters

Boolean: The resulting Boolean variable.

Variable: Any non-Boolean variable

6.7.3. Example

```
Sub CBoolExample()
    Dim sA As String, iB As Integer, iC As Boolean
    sA = "True": iB = 1
    iC = CBool(sA = "False")
    Print iC ' Prints "False"
    iC = CBool(iB)
    Print iC ' Prints "True"
End Sub
```

6.8. CDate()

Converts any data type into a Date value.

6.8.1. Syntax

```
Date = CDate(Variable)
```

6.8.2. Parameters

Boolean: The resulting date variable.

Variable: Any non-date variable

6.8.3. Example

```
Sub CDateExample()
    Dim sA As String, iB As Integer, iC As Date
    sA = "13/10/2011": iB = 32000
    iC = CDate(sA)
    Print iC ' Prints "13/10/2011"
    iC = CDate(iB)
    Print iC ' Prints "11/08/1987"
End Sub
```

6.9. Val()

Converts a string variable into a number.

6.9.1. Syntax

```
Number = Val(Variable)
```

6.9.2. Parameters

Number: The resulting numeric variable.

Variable: Any numeric string variable

6.9.3. Example

```
Sub ValExample()
    Dim sA As String, iB As Double
    sA = "100.75"
    iB = Val(sA)
    Print iB ' Prints "100.75"
End Sub
```

6.10. IsNumeric()

Checks whether a value is a number.

6.10.1. Syntax

```
Boolean = IsNumeric(Variable)
```

6.10.2. Parameters

Boolean: Indicates whether the passed variable is a number

Variable: Any variable

6.10.3. Example

```
Sub IsNumericExample()
    Dim sA As String, sB As String, bC As Boolean
    sA = "100.75": sB = "Hello"
    bC = IsNumeric(sA)
    Print bC ' Prints "True"
    bC = IsNumeric(sB)
    Print bC ' Prints "False"
End Sub
```

6.11. IsDate()

Checks whether a value is a date.

6.11.1. Syntax

```
Boolean = IsDate(Variable)
```

6.11.2. Parameters

Boolean: Indicates whether the passed variable is a date

Variable: Any variable

6.11.3. Example

```
Sub IsDateExample()
    Dim sA As String, sB As String, bC As Boolean
    sA = "13/12/2011": sB = "Hello"
    bC = IsDate(sA)
    Print bC ' Prints "True"
    bC = IsDate(sB)
    Print bC ' Prints "False"
End Sub
```

6.12. IsArray()

Checks whether a variable is an array.

6.12.1. Syntax

```
Boolean = IsArray(Variable)
```

6.12.2. Parameters

Boolean: Indicates whether the passed variable is an array

Variable: Any variable

6.12.3. Example

```
Sub IsDateExample()
    Dim sA(5) As String, sB As String, bC As Boolean
    bC = IsArray(sA)
    Print bC ' Prints "True"
    bC = IsArray(sB)
    Print bC ' Prints "False"
End Sub
```

7. String functions

OpenOffice.org Basic uses the set of Unicode characters to administer strings. Basic provides a number of functions for the conversion and manipulation of string variables.

7.1. Asc()

Returns the Unicode value of a given character.

7.1.1. Syntax

```
Code = Asc(Character)
```

7.1.2. Parameters

Code: The numeric code that is returned by the function

Character: Any single character string

7.1.3. Example

```
Sub AscExample()
    Dim iA As Integer
    iA = Asc("§")
    Print iA ' Prints "167"
End Sub
```

7.2. Chr()

Returns the character for a given Unicode value

7.2.1. Syntax

```
Character = Asc(Code)
```

7.2.2. Parameters

Code: The character represented by the Unicode value

Code: A numeric code value for the character wanted

7.2.3. Example

```
Sub ChrExample()
    Dim sA As String
    sA = Chr(199)
    Print sA ' Prints "Ç"
End Sub
```

7.3. Left()

Returns the first x characters from a string.

7.3.1. Syntax

```
ReturnedString = Left(MyString, Length)
```

7.3.2. Parameters

ReturnedString: The new shortened string returned by the function

MyString: The string to be shortened

Length: The number of characters required

7.3.3. Example

```
Sub LeftExample()
    Dim sA As String, sB As String
    sA = "Hello World"
    sB = Left(sA, 5)
    Print sB ' Prints "Hello"
End Sub
```

7.4. Right()

Returns the last x characters from a string.

7.4.1. Syntax

```
ReturnedString = Right(MyString, Length)
```

7.4.2. Parameters

ReturnedString: The new shortened string returned by the function

MyString: The string to be shortened

Length: The number of characters required

7.4.3. Example

```
Sub RightExample()
    Dim sA As String, sB As String
    sA = "Hello World"
    sB = Right(sA, 5)
    Print sB ' Prints "World"
End Sub
```

7.5. Mid()

Returns the middle x characters from a string starting at character y, can also be used to replace the middle x characters with a new set of characters.

7.5.1. Syntax

```
[ReturnedString] = Mid(MyString, Start, Length[, ReplaceString])
```

7.5.2. Parameters

ReturnedString: The new shortened string returned by the function. If the replacement capability is used then no value is returned.

MyString: The string to be shortened

Start: The character to start from

Length: The number of characters required

ReplaceString: The new string to be used to replace the selected characters. This is an optional parameter.

7.5.3. Example

```
Sub MidExample()
    Dim sA As String, sB As String
    sA = "Hello World"
    sB = Mid(sA, 4, 4)
    Mid(sA, 7, 5, "Mum")
    Print sA + " " + sB ' Prints "Hello Mum loW"
End Sub
```

7.6. Len()

Returns the number of characters in a string.

7.6.1. Syntax

```
Length = Len(MyString)
```

7.6.2. Parameters

Length: The number of characters in the string

MyString: The string to be measured

7.6.3. Example

```
Sub LenExample()
    Dim sA As String, iB As Integer
    sA = "Hello World"
    iB = Len(sA)
    Print iB ' Prints "11"
End Sub
```

7.7. InStr()

Searches for a sub-string within a string.

7.7.1. Syntax

```
FoundPosition = InStr(MyString, SearchString)
```

7.7.2. Parameters

FoundPosition: The position at which the sub-string is found or 0 if not found.

MyString: The string to be searched.

SearchString: The string to be looked for

7.7.3. Example

```
Sub InStrExample()
    Dim sA As String, iB As Integer
    sA = "Hello World"
    iB = InStr(sA, "Wo")
    Print iB ' Prints "7"
End Sub
```

7.8. Format()

Converts a number into a string using the format given.

7.8.1. Syntax

```
String = Format(Number, FormatString)
```

7.8.2. Parameters

String: The created string representing the number in the correct format.

Number: The number to be converted.

FormatString: The format that is to be applied.

7.8.3. Example

```
Sub FormatExample()
    Dim sA As String, iB As Double
    ib = 1234.5
    sA = Format(iB, "#,##0.00")
    Print sA ' Prints "1,234.50"
    sA = Format(iB, "$#,##0.00")
    Print sA ' Prints "$1,234.50"
End Sub
```

8. Date and time functions

8.1. DateSerial()

Converts 3 numbers into a date using the format defined by the locale.

8.1.1. Syntax

```
Date = DateSerial(Year, Month, Day)
```

8.1.2. Parameters

Date: The created date variable.

Year: The number representing the year.

Month: The number representing the month.

Day: The number representing the day.

8.1.3. Example

```
Sub DateSerialExample()
    Dim dA As Date
    dA = DateSerial(2001, 12, 13)
    Print dA ' Prints "13/12/2001"
End Sub
```

8.2. TimeSerial()

Converts 3 numbers into a time using the format defined by the locale.

8.2.1. Syntax

```
Time = TimeSerial(Hour, Minute, Second)
```

8.2.2. Parameters

Time: The created time variable.
Hour: The number representing the hour.
Minute: The number representing the minutes.
Second: The number representing the seconds.

8.2.3. Example

```
Sub TimeSerialExample()
    Dim dA As Date
    dA = TimeSerial(20, 15, 25)
    Print dA ' Prints "20:15:25"
End Sub
```

8.3. Day()

Returns the day of the month from a date.

8.3.1. Syntax

```
Day = Day(Date)
```

8.3.2. Parameters

Day: The day of the month.

Date: The date to be processed.

8.3.3. Example

```
Sub DayExample()
    Dim iA As Integer
    iA = Day("12/07/2012")
    Print iA ' Prints "12"
End Sub
```

8.4. Month()

Returns the month from a date.

8.4.1. Syntax

```
Month = Month(Date)
```

8.4.2. Parameters

Month: The month returned.

Date: The date to be processed.

8.4.3. Example

```
Sub MonthExample()
    Dim iA As Integer
    iA = Day("12/07/2012")
    Print iA ' Prints "7"
End Sub
```

8.5. Year()

Returns the year from a date.

8.5.1. Syntax

```
Year = Year(Date)
```

8.5.2. Parameters

Year: The year returned.

Date: The date to be processed.

8.5.3. Example

```
Sub YearExample()
    Dim iA As Integer
    iA = Day("12/07/2012")
    Print iA ' Prints "2012"
End Sub
```

8.6. Weekday()

Returns the number of the day of the week from a date.

8.6.1. Syntax

```
Weekday = Weekday(Date)
```

8.6.2. Parameters

Weekday: The number representing the day of the week that is returned.

Date: The date to be processed.

8.6.3. Example

```
Sub WeekdayExample()
    Dim iA As Integer
    iA = Weekday("12/07/2012")
    Print iA ' Prints "5"
End Sub
```

8.7. Hour()

Returns the hour from a time.

8.7.1. Syntax

```
Hour = Hour(Time)
```

8.7.2. Parameters

Hour: The hour returned.

Time: The time to be processed.

8.7.3. Example

```
Sub HourExample()
    Dim iA As Integer
    iA = Hour("21:07:35")
    Print iA ' Prints "21"
End Sub
```

8.8. Minute()

Returns the minutes from a time.

8.8.1. Syntax

```
Minutes = Minute(Time)
```

8.8.2. Parameters

Minutes: The minutes returned.

Time: The time to be processed.

8.8.3. Example

```
Sub MinuteExample()
    Dim iA As Integer
    iA = Minute("21:07:35")
    Print iA ' Prints "7"
End Sub
```

8.9. Second()

Returns the seconds from a time.

8.9.1. Syntax

```
Seconds = Second(Time)
```

8.9.2. Parameters

Seconds: The seconds returned.

Time: The time to be processed.

8.9.3. Example

```
Sub SecondExample()
    Dim iA As Integer
    iA = Second("21:07:35")
    Print iA ' Prints "35"
End Sub
```

8.10. Date()

Returns the present date as a string. The format depends on locale settings

8.10.1. Syntax

```
Date = Date()
```

8.10.2. Parameters

Date: The date string returned.

8.10.3. Example

```
Sub DateExample()
    Dim sA As String
    sA = Date()
    Print sA ' Prints "11/08/2012"
End Sub
```

8.11. Time()

Returns the present time as a string.

8.11.1. Syntax

```
Time = Time()
```

8.11.2. Parameters

Time: The time string returned.

8.11.3. Example

```
Sub TimeExample()
    Dim sA As String
    sA = Time()
    Print sA ' Prints "15:39:21"
End Sub
```

8.12. Now()

Returns the present time and date as a Date variable.

8.12.1. Syntax

```
TimeDate = Now()
```

8.12.2. Parameters

TimeDate: The date variable returned.

8.12.3. Example

```
Sub NowExample()
    Dim dA As Date
    dA = Now()
    Print dA ' Prints "11/08/2012 15:41:14"
End Sub
```

9. File and directory functions

OpenOffice.org Basic provides two means of interacting with files. Firstly, through the API, which provides a whole range of objects with which you can create and modify Office documents. Secondly, you can directly access the file system, using the functions described below.

9.1. CompatabilityMode()

Compatibility mode provides greater compatibility with VBA, by changing the operation of some functions.

9.1.1. Syntax

```
[Mode] = CompatabilityMode([OnOff])
```

9.1.2. Parameters

Mode: Optional return value if the OnOff argument is not given – used for getting the mode.

OnOff: Boolean value, used for setting the compatibility mode.

9.1.3. Example

```
Sub CompatabilityModeExample()
    Dim bA As Boolean
    bA = CompatabilityMode()
    Print bA ' Prints "False"
End Sub
```

9.2. Dir()

Searches through directories for files and sub-directories.

9.2.1. Syntax

```
FileName = Dir[(Directory, FileDir)]
```

9.2.2. Parameters

FileName: The name of the file found.

Directory: The directory to be searched – optional parameter, only needed the first time of calling in a macro.

FileDir: Specifies whether to search for files (0) or sub-directories (16)

9.2.3. Example

```
Sub DirExample()
    Dim sA As String
    sA = Dir("C:\", 0)
    Print sA ' Prints "bootmgr"
    sA = Dir
    Print sA ' Prints "BOOTSECT.BAK"
End Sub
```

9.3. MkDir()

Creates the specified directory

9.3.1. Syntax

```
MkDir(DirName)
```

9.3.2. Parameters

DirName: The name of the directory to be created. All directories within the hierarchy are also created if they don't exist.

9.3.3. Example

```
Sub MkDirExample()
    MkDir("C:\TempDir\TempDir2")
End Sub
```

9.4. RmDir()

Removes the specified directory

9.4.1. Syntax

```
RmDir(DirName)
```

9.4.2. Parameters

DirName: The name of the directory to be removed. Care needs to be taken, as all sub-directories and files in the directory will also be deleted

9.4.3. Example

```
Sub RmDirExample()
    RmDir("C:\TempDir\TempDir2")
End Sub
```

9.5. FileCopy()

Copies a file

9.5.1. Syntax

```
FileCopy(OriginalFile, CopyFile)
```

9.5.2. Parameters

OriginalFile: The name of the file to be copied

CopyFile: The name of the new file to be copied to

9.5.3. Example

```
Sub FileCopyExample()
    FileCopy("spreadsheet.ods", "copy_spreadsheet.ods")
End Sub
```

9.6. Name

Renames a file

9.6.1. Syntax

```
Name OldName As NewName
```

9.6.2. Parameters

OldName: The name of the file to be renamed

NewName: The new name of the file

9.6.3. Example

```
Sub NameExample()
    Name "spreadsheet.ods" AS "new_spreadsheet.ods"
End Sub
```

9.7. Kill()

Deletes a file

9.7.1. Syntax

```
Kill(FileName)
```

9.7.2. Parameters

FileName: The name of the file to be deleted

9.7.3. Example

```
Sub KillExample()
    Kill("spreadsheet.ods")
End Sub
```

9.8. FileExists()

Checks whether a file exists or not

9.8.1. Syntax

```
CheckExists = FileExists(FileName)
```

9.8.2. Parameters

CheckExists: Boolean indicating whether the file exists or not.

FileName: The name of the file to be checked

9.8.3. Example

```
Sub FileExistsExample()
    If FileExists("spreadsheet.ods") Then
        MsgBox "The file spreadsheet.ods exists."
    End If
End Sub
```

9.9. GetAttr()

Get some properties about the file

9.9.1. Syntax

```
Attr = GetAttr(FileName)
```

9.9.2. Parameters

Attr: The attribute returned. This is returned as a Integer bit mask, with the possible values 1 (read-only) and 16 (directory)

FileName: The name of the file to get properties for

9.9.3. Example

```
Sub GetAttrExample()
    FileMask = GetAttr("spreadsheed.ods")
    If (FileMask AND 1) > 0 Then
        FileDescription = "Read-only "
    End If
    If (FileMask AND 16) > 0 Then
        FileDescription = FileDescription + "directory"
    End If
    If FileDescription = "" Then
        FileDescription = "normal"
    End If
    MsgBox FileDescription
End Sub
```

9.10. SetAttr()

Sets the Attributes of a file

9.10.1. Syntax

```
SetAttr(FileName, Attr)
```

9.10.2. Parameters

FileName: The name of the file to be updated

Attr: The attribute to be set

9.10.3. Example

```
Sub SetAttrExample()
    ' First set the file to be read-only
    SetAttr("spreadsheet.ods", 1)
    ' Now remove the read-only status of the file
    SetAttr("spreadsheet.ods", 0)
End Sub
```

9.11. FileDateTime()

Returns the date and time that the file was last modified.

9.11.1. Syntax

```
FileDateTime(FileName)
```

9.11.2. Parameters

FileName: The name of the file to be read

9.11.3. Example

```
Sub FileDateTimeExample()
    MsgBox FileDateTime("spreadsheet.ods")
End Sub
```

9.12. FileLen()

Returns the length of the file.

9.12.1. Syntax

```
FileLen(FileName)
```

9.12.2. Parameters

FileName: The name of the file to be updated

9.12.3. Example

```
Sub FileLenExample()
    MsgBox FileLen("spreadsheet.ods")
End Sub
```

9.13. FreeFile

Before a (non-OpenOffice document) file can be opened and worked with, it needs to have a file handle assigned to it.

9.13.1. Syntax

```
FileNo = FreeFile
```

9.13.2. Parameters

FileNo: An integer that receives the file handle

9.13.3. Example

```
Sub FreeFileExample()
    FileNo = FreeFile
    Open "test.txt" For Output As FileNo
    Close #FileNo
End Sub
```

9.14. Open

Once a file handle has been assigned, a file must be opened before it can be worked on. A file is either opened for input or for output, depending on whether you want to read it or write to it.

9.14.1. Syntax

```
Open FileName For Input | Output As FileNo
```

9.14.2. Parameters

FileName: The name of the file to be opened

FileNo: the file handle that was assigned using FreeFile

9.14.3. Example

```
Sub OpenExample()
    FileNo = FreeFile
    Open "test.txt" For Output As FileNo
    Close #FileNo
End Sub
```

9.15. Close

Once you have finished writing to or reading from a file, you should close it.

9.15.1. Syntax

```
Open #FileNo
```

9.15.2. Parameters

FileNo: the file handle that was assigned using FreeFile

9.15.3. Example

```
Sub CloseExample()
    FileNo = FreeFile
    Open "test.txt" For Output As FileNo
    Close #FileNo
End Sub
```

9.16. Print

If you have opened your file for output, then you can use the Print instruction to output data to the file.

9.16.1. Syntax

```
Print #FileNo, OutputData
```

9.16.2. Parameters

FileNo: the file handle that was assigned using FreeFile

OutputData: The data to be output to the file

9.16.3. Example

```
Sub PrintExample()
    FileNo = FreeFile
    Open "test.txt" For Output As FileNo
    Print #FileNo, "Hello World"
    Close #FileNo
End Sub
```

9.17. Line Input

If you have opened your file for input, then you can use the Line Input instruction to read data from the file.

9.17.1. Syntax

```
Line Input #FileNo, InputData
```

9.17.2. Parameters

FileNo: The file handle that was assigned using FreeFile

InputData: Variable where the data read from the is stored

9.17.3. Example

```
Sub LineInputExample()
    FileNo = FreeFile
    Open "test.txt" For Input As FileNo
    Do While Not Eof(FileNo)
        Line Input #FileNo, InputData
        TextString = TextString & InputData & Chr(13)
    Loop
    Close #FileNo
    MsgBox TextString
End Sub
```

9.18. Eof()

When you are reading data from a file, you need to be able to check whether you have reached the end of the file. This is done using the Eof() instruction.

9.18.1. Syntax

```
EndReached = Eof(FileNo)
```

9.18.2. Parameters

FileNo: The file handle that was assigned using FreeFile

EndReached: A Boolean value indicating whether the end of the file has been reached.

9.18.3. Example

```
Sub LineInputExample()
    FileNo = FreeFile
    Open "test.txt" For Input As FileNo

    Do While Not Eof(FileNo)
        Line Input #FileNo, InputData
        TextString = TextString & InputData & Chr(13)
    Loop

    Close #FileNo
    MsgBox TextString
End Sub
```

10. Messages and Input Boxes

10.1. MsgBox()

MsgBox displays information in a message box, along with one or more buttons to click.

10.1.1. Syntax

ReturnValue = MsgBox TextString, [ButtonSelection[, TitleString]]

10.1.2. Parameters

ReturnValue: Integer value representing the button that was pressed. Returns the following values:

- 1, IDOK – OK button was pressed
- 2, IDCANCEL – Cancel button was pressed
- 3, IDABORT – Abort button was pressed
- 4, IDRETRY – Retry button was pressed
- 6, IDYES – Yes button was pressed
- 7, IDNO – The No button was pressed

TextString: The information to be displayed in the message box

ButtonSelect: An Integer value representing the buttons and icon to be displayed. Can take the following values:

- 0, MB_OK – Display the OK button
- 1, MB_OKCANCEL – Display the OK and Cancel buttons
- 2, MB_ABORTRETRYIGNORE – Display the Abort, Retry and Ignore buttons
- 3, MB_YESNOCANCEL – Display the Yes, No and Cancel buttons
- 4, MB_YESNO – Display the Yes and No buttons
- 5, MB_RETRYCANCEL – Display the Retry and Cancel buttons
- 16, MB_ICONSTOP – Display the stop sign icon
- 32, MB_ICONQUESTION – Display the question mark icon
- 48, MB_ICONEXCLAMATION – Display the exclamation mark icon
- 64, MB_ICONINFORMATION – Display the tip icon
- 256, MB_DEFBUTTON2 – The second button is the default
- 512, MB_DEFBUTTON3 – The third button is the default

10.1.3. Example 1

```
Sub MsgBoxExample1()
    MsgBox "This is a simple message box"
End Sub
```

This code will display the following message box

10.1.4. Example 2

```
Sub MsgBoxExample2()
    iButtons = MB_YESNO + MB_DEFBUTTON2 + MB_ICONQUESTION
    MessageString = "Do you want to continue?"
    If MsgBox(MessageString, iButtons, "System Message") = IDNO Then
        Exit Sub
    End If
    ...
End Sub
```

This code will display the following message box

10.2. InputBox()

InputBox displays a simple message box with a field for a user to enter a value.

10.2.1. Syntax

EnteredString = InputBox(TextString, TitleString, DefaultValue)

10.2.2. Parameters

EnteredString: The string entered by the user

TextString: The information to be displayed in the input box

TitleString: The title of the input box

DefaultValue: The default value to be shown in the text entry field

10.2.3. Example

```
Sub InputBoxExample()
    MessageString = InputBox("This is a simple input box", "Input Box", "Default Value")
End Sub
```

This code will display the following input box

11.   Other functions

11.1.   Beep

Plays a sound to warn the user of an incorrect action.

11.1.1.   Syntax

```
Beep
```

11.1.2.   Parameters

11.1.3.   Example

```
Sub BeepExample()
   Beep
End Sub
```

11.2.   Shell()

Run an external program

11.2.1.   Syntax

```
Shell(PathName, WindowStyle, Params, bSync)
```

11.2.2.   Parameters

PathName: The name and path of the command to be run

WindowStyle: The style of the window that the program is to be run in:

- 0 – Program receives focus and starts in a concealed window
- 1 – Program receives focus and starts in a normal-sized window
- 2 – Program receives focus and starts in a minimized window
- 3 – Program receives focus and starts in a maximized window
- 4 – Program starts in a normal-sized window without focus
- 6 – Program starts in a minimized window without focus
- 10 -Program starts in full screen mode

Param: Command line parameters to be passed to the program

bSync: A Boolean that indicates whether OpenOffice.org Basic should wait for the shell command to finish before continuing

11.2.3. Example

```
Sub ShellExample()
    Shell("c:\windows\system32\calc.exe", 2, "", True)
End Sub
```

11.3. Wait

Pause for a specified period

11.3.1. Syntax

```
Wait TimeLength
```

11.3.2. Parameters

TimeLength: The length of time in milliseconds to pause for (1000 = 1 second)

11.3.3. Example

```
Sub WaitExample()
    Wait 10000
End Sub
```

11.4. WaitUntil

Wait until a certain time

11.4.1. Syntax

```
WaitUntil WaitTime
```

11.4.2. Parameters

WaitTime: A Date variable that specifies the time to wait until

11.4.3. Example

```
Sub WaitUntilExample()
    WaitUntil Now + TimeValue("00:01:00")
End Sub
```

11.5. Environ()

Get a system environment variable

11.5.1. Syntax

```
ReturnString = Environ(VarName)
```

11.5.2. Parameters

ReturnString: The details of the variable requested

VarName: The name of the variable to get

11.5.3. Example

```
Sub EnvironExample()
    Environ("TEMP")
End Sub
```

12. The OpenOfffice.org API

12.1. Introduction

OpenOffice.org objects and methods, such as paragraphs, spreadsheets, and fonts, are accessible to OpenOffice.org Basic through the Application Programming Interface, or API. Through the API, for example, spreadsheets can be created, opened, modified and printed. The interface between the API and various programming languages is provided by Universal Network Objects (UNO).

This chapter provides an introduction into the API. Building on this background, subsequent chapters will show how the API can be used with different types of documents to make OpenOffice.org do what you want it to do.

12.2. Universal Network Objects (UNO)

OpenOffice.org supplies a programming interface in the form of the Universal Network Objects (UNO). This is an object-oriented programming interface which is sub-divided into various objects, which provide access to the various functions of the OpenOffice package.

To use a Universal Network Object in OpenOffice.org Basic, you first need a variable declaration for the associated object. The declaration is made using the Dim instruction. The Object type designation should be used to declare an object variable:

```
Dim ObjName As Object
```

Once you have your object variable declared, it must be initialised, before it can be used. The initialisation is performed using the createUNOService function as follows:

```
ObjName = createUNOService("com.sun.star.frame.Desktop")
```

This call assigns a reference to the newly created object to the Obj variable. While com.sun.star.frame.Desktop resembles an object type; in UNO terminology it is called a service rather than a type. In accordance with UNO philosophy, an Obj is described as a reference to an object which supports the com.sun.star.frame.Desktop service.

Some UNO services in turn support other services so that, through one object, you are provided with access to a whole range of services. For example, the com.sun.star.frame.Desktop service, can also include other services for loading documents and for ending the program.

12.3. API Properties and methods

Objects in OpenOffice.org Basic provide a range of properties and methods which can be called by means of the object.

12.3.1. Properties

Properties are the definition of information that is held by an object. For example, if you create a document object it will have properties such as Title and Filename. Like variables, properties have a type, which defines what values it can hold. The properties are set using a simple assignment

```
Document.Title = "OpenOffice.org Basic – an Introduction"
```

12.3.2. Methods

Methods can be thought of as functions that call the object and relate directly to that object. For example, the Document object previously mentioned might have a Save method, which would be called as follows

```
Document.Save()
```

Methods also support parameters and return values, just like functions. For example, the following snippet specifies a True parameter for the Save method and stores the return value in the Response variable

```
Response = Document.Save(True)
```

12.4. Modules and services

OpenOffice.org contains a large number of services, which can be thought of as objects. These objects are organised into modules – where each module contains a number of related services. To access an individual service, you must know its full name including the module that it is in. The name is in the format shown below:

```
com.sun.star.<module>.<service>
```

where "com.sun.star" is a constant expression that specifies that it is an OpenOffice.org service. For example, to access the SortField service, which is part of the util module you would use the following:

```
com.sun.star.util.SortField
```

12.5. Identifying methods and properties

In order to work with the API, you need to be able to identify which methods and properties are supported by which services. There are a number of ways of doing this, which are detailed below.

12.5.1. The supportsservice Method

The supportsservice method is supported by a number of UNO objects, and can be used to establish whether an object supports a particular service. For example, the following call can determine whether the Element object supports the com.sun.star.TextGraphicObject service:

```
Response = Element.supportsService("com.sun.star.text.TextGraphicObject")
```

The method will return True if the service is supported by the object.

12.5.2. Debug properties

OpenOffice.org Basic provides a number of properties that return the details of which properties, methods and interfaces an object contains. The following are the relevant properties:

- DBG_properties – returns a string with all the properties of an object.
- DBG_methods – returns a string with all the methods of an object.
- DBG_supportedInterfaces – returns a string with all the interfaces that support the object.

The following code shows the properties, methods and interfaces supported by the Desktop service:

```
Sub ShowServiceDetails()
    Dim Obj As Object
    Obj = createUnoService("com.sun.star.frame.Desktop")

    MsgBox Obj.DBG_Properties
    MsgBox Obj.DBG_methods
    MsgBox Obj.DBG_supportedInterfaces
End Sub
```

It should be noted though that DBG_properties returns all the properties that the services offered by the object can theoretically support. However, it is not definite proof that the property can be used by the object in question, so it is always safer to use the IsEmpty function to check if it is actually available.

12.5.3. API Reference

Details of the available services and their interfaces, methods and properties can be found in either the OpenOffice.org API reference (http://api.openoffice.org/docs/common/ref/com/sun/star/module-ix.html.

13. Working with OpenOffice.org Documents

The remainder of this book will deal with the interfaces and services that are available for dealing with the different types of documents that the OpenOffice.org suite provides. This chapter will deal with those function areas that are common across all the different types of documents, such as opening, saving and printing documents. Subsequent chapters will deal with functions that relate to a specific document type.

13.1. The StarDesktop

Two services are commonly used when working with OpenOffice.org documents:

- The com.sun.star.frame.Desktop service provides all the functions for the frame object of OpenOffice.org, under which all the document windows are stored. Using this service, documents can be created, opened and imported.
- The com.sun.star.document.OfficeDocument service provides functionality for the individual documents. This service allows you to save, export and print documents.

The com.sun.star.frame.Desktop service can be accessed using the global name StarDesktop. Another important global name is ThisComponent, which refers to the active OpenOffice.org document.

13.2. Document information

13.2.1. URL notation

As OpenOffice.org is platform independent, it uses URL notation for defining file names. The notation using this system means that filenames start with the prefix file:///, followed by the path to the file. It should be noted that this notation uses forward slashes, not the back slashes normally used under Windows. Therefore, to access the file C:\documents\test.odt, the following path would be used – file:///C:/documents/test.odt.

To aid the conversion between local file names and URL notation, OpenOffice.org provides two functions. ConvertToUrl converts a local filename into an URL and ConvertFromUrl converts an URL into a local filename.

The Internet Standard RFC1738, which defines the structure of URLs permits the use of characters 0-9, a-z and A-Z. All other characters are inserted using escape coding as their hexadecimal value preceded by a percent sign. Thus a space in the local filename becomes %20 in the URL.

13.2.2. XML file format

OpenOffice.org documents are stored in a format that is based on XML, which means that they can in principle be opened and edited with a text editor. However, in order to cut down on the space required for the storage of the files, OpenOffice.org compresses them using a zip algorithm. It is however possible to specify be means of an option in the **storeAsURL** method that the file be stored in its uncompressed format.

13.3. Creating and loading documents

Documents are created and opened using the **loadComponentFromURL** method. This method has the following construction:

NewComponent = StarDesktop.loadComponentFromURL(URL, Frame, SearchFlags, Properties)

URL is the filename of the file to be loaded in URL notation. For creating a new document, the URL is set to "private:factory/scalc", "private:factory/swriter", etc depending upon the type of document to be created.

Frame specifies the frame object that the document should be loaded into. This can either be set to the name of an existing frame or to "_blank" to specify that a new frame should be created.

SearchFlags specifies how to find the frame name and can take the following values:

Value	Constant	Description
0	AUTO	Search for nothing – commonly used with new frames.
1	PARENT	Search the parent frames.
2	SELF	Include the start frame itself.
4	CHILDREN	Includes all the child frames of the start frame.
8	CREATE	If the frame cannot be found then create it.
16	SIBLINGS	Include the direct siblings of the current frame.
32	TASKS	Search outside of the current sub-task tree.
23	ALL	Include all frames except other tasks sub trees.
55	GLOBAL	Search the entire hierarchy of frames.

Properties is used to provide arguments that specify component or filter behaviour. For example, to open a document read-only, the argument "ReadOnly" with a value of True would be used. A full list of the options that are available can be found in Appendix I

The return value NewComponent returns either a Document object if the document loaded successfully or Null if it failed.

The following code will load the document test.odt read-only into a new frame

```
Dim oDoc As Object
Dim sURL As String
Dim Properties(0) As New com.sun.star.beans.PropertyValue

Properties(0).Name = "ReadOnly"
Properties(0).Value = True

sURL = "file:///C:/documents/test.odt"

oDoc = StarDesktop.loadComponentFromURL(sURL, "_blank", 0, Properties())
```

To load the document into a named frame, only one line needs to be added, and another changed, as follows:

```
SearchFlags = com.sun.star.frame.FrameSearchFlag.CREATE + _
              com.sun.star.frame.FrameSearchFlag.ALL

oDoc = StarDesktop.loadComponentFromURL(sURL, "MyFrame", SearchFlags, Properties())
```

13.4. Saving documents

The Document object is used to save documents, using the store() and storeAsURL() methods. The store method can be used when a document already has been previously saved or loaded and the storeAsURL method is used for new documents that don't have a file location associated with them. The two methods are called as follows:

```
oDoc.store()
oDoc.storeAsURL(URL, Arguments)
```

The arguments that can be used with the storeAsURL function can be found in Appendix II.

The document object also provides some other useful methods for use when saving a document:

- hasLocation() specifies whether the document has already been assigned a URL.
- isReadonly() specifies whether a document is read-only or not.
- isModified() specifies whether a document has been modified since it was last saved.

Using all of these methods, the following code can be used for correctly saving a document:

```
If (oDoc.isModified) Then
    If (oDoc.hasLocation And (Not oDoc.isReadOnly)) Then
        oDoc.store()
    Else
        oDoc.storeAsURL(sURL, Dummy())
    End If
End If
```

The code first checks to see whether the document has been modified since it was last saved and only continues the saving process if it has. It then checks whether the document has already been assigned a URL and that it is not read-only and if this is the case saves it under the existing URL, otherwise it saves it under a new URL.

13.5. Printing documents

Printing of documents is also performed using the Document object. The object includes a Print method, which at its simplest will print all the pages of a document. As with the load and saving methods, there are additional options that can be specified as a parameter for the Print method, these can be seen in Appendix III. Here is an example of printing out a specified set of pages using the Pages option:

```
Dim PrintProperties(1) As New com.sun.star.beans.PropertyValue

PrintProperties(0).Name = "Pages"
PrintProperties(0).Value = "1-2; 5-8; 10"
PrintProperties(1).Name = "Wait"
PrintProperties(1).Value = True
oDoc.Print(PrintProperties())
```

13.5.1. Printer selection

OpenOffice.org additionally allows you to select which printer to print to and set the settings for that printer. This is done through the Printer property of a document object. The settings that can be applied are listed in Appendix III. The example below sets the printer name and the size of the paper to use:

```
Dim oDoc As Object
Dim PrinterProperties(1) As New com.sun.star.beans.PropertyValue
Dim PaperSize As New com.sun.star.awt.Size

PaperSize.Width = 20000          ' equals to 20 cm
PaperSize.Height = 20000         ' equals to 20 cm
PrinterProperties(0).Name = "Name"
PrinterProperties(0).Value = "My HP Laserjet"
PrinterProperties(1).Name = "PaperSize"
PrinterProperties(1).Value = PaperSize
oDoc.Printer = PrinterProperties()
```

13.6. Styles

Styles hold details about formatting attributes and make it easier to keep formatting within a document consistent. Styles allow you to change an attribute such as the font and then all occurrences of that style in the document are updated.

13.6.1. Style types

OpenOffice.org recognises different types of styles depending on the type of document that is being used.

Writer recognises the following types of styles:

•Character styles
•Paragraph styles
•Frame styles
•Page styles
•Numbering styles

Calc recognises the following types of styles:

•Cell styles
•Page styles

Impress recognises the following types of styles:

•Character element styles
•Presentation styles

The different types of styles are referred to as StyleFamilies and are accessed as a property of a Document object. Within each StyleFamily, there are methods for interacting with the individual styles. The following macro uses the StyleFamilies property to get all the Page styles of a text document and then displays the names of the individual styles:

```
Sub ShowPageStyles()
    Dim oDoc As Object
    Dim Sheet As Object
    Dim StyleFamilies As Object
    Dim CellStyles As Object
    Dim CellStyle As Object
    Dim I As Integer
    Dim sOutputString As String

    oDoc = ThisComponent
    StyleFamilies = oDoc.StyleFamilies
    CellStyles = StyleFamilies.getByName("PageStyles")

    For I = 0 To CellStyles.Count - 1
      CellStyle = CellStyles(I)
      sOutputString = sOutputString & CellStyle.Name & Chr(13)
    Next I
    MsgBox sOutputString
End Sub
```

13.7.   Templates

Templates are models that you can use to create other documents. For example, you might create a template of a letter with your name and address already in position at the top of the letter. Each time you create a document based on a template, it will include all the details included in that template. If you develop code and store it in a template, then it will also be available for any document that is based on that template.

Templates are associated with a particular document type, and any code that is designed for a document will also work with templates of that particular document type.

14. Text documents (Writer)

14.1. Introduction

Text documents are created in OpenOffice.org using the Writer application. These documents include not just text, but also the formatting instructions for that text and also object such as illustrations and charts. This formatting and insertion of objects can take place anywhere within the document.

This chapter deals with the interfaces and services that are specific to text documents. First we will look at the structure of text documents, such as paragraphs and formatting. In the second part of the chapter, we will look at how OpenOffice.org Basic can help you in the editing of text document. Finally, we will look beyond text and deal with tables, bookmarks, frames and more.

14.2. The structure of text documents

This section concentrates on the actual text and associated formatting options for a text document.

The fundamental layout of a text document is that of a sequence of paragraphs. These paragraphs do not have any reference or index, so it is not possible to directly access a particular paragraph. However, what can be achieved is a sequential transverse of the paragraphs using the Enumeration object.

The Enumeration object will return all paragraphs and tables in a document, and it is therefore necessary to check whether a returned object supports the com.sun.star.Paragraph or com.sun.star.TextTable services to determine whether you are dealing with a paragraph or a table.

The code on the next page loops through the contents of a text document and displays a message to identify whether each text block is a paragraph or a table.

```
Dim oEnum As Object
Dim oTextElement As Object

' Create enumeration object
oEnum = ThisComponent.Text.createEnumeration

' loop over all text elements
While oEnum.hasMoreElements
    oTextElement = oEnum.nextElement

    If oTextElement.supportsService("com.sun.star.text.TextTable") Then
        MsgBox "The current block contains a table."
    End If

    If oTextElement.supportsService("com.sun.star.text.Paragraph") Then
        MsgBox "The current block contains a paragraph."
    End If
Wend
```

The code creates an Enumeration object from the current document and then loops through all the elements of the Enumeration object, checking each one to see which of the Paragraph and TextTable services it supports and displays a message as applicable.

14.3. Paragraphs

Once you have identified an element as being a paragraph, you can access the text in the paragraph using the String property of the Element. The example below loops through the elements in a document and if they are a paragraph, displays the text in a message box.

```
Dim oEnum As Object
Dim oTextElement As Object

' Create enumeration object
oEnum = ThisComponent.Text.createEnumeration

' loop over all text elements
While oEnum.hasMoreElements
    oTextElement = oEnum.nextElement
    If oTextElement.supportsService("com.sun.star.text.Paragraph") Then
        MsgBox oTextElement.String
    End If
Wend
```

14.4. Paragraph portions

When using the String property of a Paragraph, one has to be careful if you are replacing parts of the text, as it may result in the loss of formatting. This is because a paragraph consists of a number of sub-objects, each with its own formatting information. For example, if a paragraph contains a word in the middle in red, then the paragraph will be stored in OpenOffice.org as three paragraph portions: the portion before the red word, the red word and the portion after the red word. If you replace a string, then the formatting of that portion is lost.

To enable you to access these individual portions, paragraphs provide their own Enumeration object, which allows you to loop through the portions of a paragraph one by one and interact with the text of each individual portion.

If you wish to navigate at a lower level than paragraph portions then you will need to use a TextCursor, which will be covered later in the book.

14.5. Formatting

Within OpenOffice.org, text can be formatted in two ways – direct formatting and indirect formatting.

- Direct formatting is achieved by highlighting a section of text (for example a word) and applying the format, such as **bold**.
- Indirect formatting is achieved by using a style, for example marking a section of text as Heading 1 will apply all the formatting associated with the style to the section of text.

There are a number of formatting properties associated with character and paragraph level formatting. A full list of the character and paragraph properties can be found online at the OpenOffice.org API reference. The most important ones are described below.

14.5.1. Character properties

Character properties are properties that can be applied to individual characters, such as font type and underline type. Objects that allow character properties to be set support the com.star.sun.style.CharacterProperties service. The properties are set using a number of properties offered by the CharacterProperties service. Here are some of the important character properties:

- CharFontName (String) – name of font type selected.
- CharColor (Long) – text colour.
- CharHeight (Float) – character height in points (pt).
- CharUnderline (Constant group) – type of underscore (constants defined in com.sun.star.awt.FontUnderline).
- CharWeight (Constant group) – font weight (defined in com.sun.star.awt.FontWeight).
- CharBackColor (Long) – background colour.
- CharKeepTogether (Boolean) – suppression of automatic line break.
- CharStyleName (String) – name of character template.

14.5.2. Paragraph properties

Formatting that is not applied to individual characters, but to paragraphs as a whole are considered to be a paragraph property. These are properties such as indents and line spacing. Any object that supports the com.sun.star.text.Paragraph service also supports the application of paragraph properties using the com.sun.star.style.ParagraphProperties service. The most common paragraph properties are:

- ParaAdjust (enum) – vertical text orientation (defined in com.sun.star.style.ParagraphAdjust).
- ParaLineSpacing (struct) – line spacing (structure in accordance with com.sun.star.style.LineSpacing).
- ParaBackColor (Long) – background colour.
- ParaLeftMargin (Long) – left margin in 100ths of a millimetre.
- ParaRightMargin (Long) – right margin in 100ths of a millimetre.
- ParaTopMargin (Long) – top margin in 100ths of a millimetre.
- ParaBottomMargin (Long) – bottom margin in 100ths of a millimetre.
- ParaTabStops (Array of struct) – type and position of tabs (array with structures of the type com.sun.star.style.TabStop).
- ParaStyleName (String) – name of the paragraph template.

14.5.3. Direct or indirect formatting?

Direct formatting takes priority over indirect formatting, so for example if a paragraph is indirectly formatted using a style that is bold and one word is directly formatted to not be bold, then that word will be unbolded. However, if a style is applied after direct formatting then it will replace the direct formatting.

It can be difficult to determine whether a section has been formatted directly or indirectly. However, OpenOffice.org basic provides the getPropertyState() method, which can be used to get information about how a property was set. This method returns one of three values:

- com.sun.star.beans.PropertyState.DIRECT_VALUE, which indicates that the property was defined by direct formatting.
- com.sun.star.beans.PropertyState.DEFAULT_VALUE, which indicates that the property was defined indirectly by a template.
- com.sun.star.beans.PropertyState.AMBIGUOUS_VALUE, which indicates that the formatting origin is unclear.

14.6. The TextCursor

TextCursors mark a particular point in a text document and can be thought of as analogous to the cursor used in OpenOffice. They can be used to provide methods for changing text and navigating within a text document.

14.6.1. Naviating with a TextCursor

Whilst the TextCursor is similar to the visible cursor in a text document, it is not the same thing. Moving the location of a TextCursor does not affect the positioning of the actual cursor in a document. You can also have several TextCursor objects in existence for the same document.

TextCursors are created using the createTextCursor() method as follows:

```
Dim oCursor As Object
oCursor = ThisComponent.Text.createTextCursor()
```

The TextCursor object supports the com.sun.star.text.TextCursor service, which provides a number of methods for navigating within text documents, which can be seen in Appendix IV.

As an example, the following code will move the TextCursor to the 10th character of the current sentence:

```
oCursor.gotoStartOfSentence(False)
oCursor.goRight(10, False)
```

In addition to the navigation methods, the TextCursor also provides a selection of methods for unhighlighting a section:

- collapseToStart() – cancels the highlighting and moves the cursor to the start of the selection that was previously highlighted.
- collapseToEnd() – cancels the highlighting and moves the cursor to the end of the selection that was previously highlighted.
- isCollapsed() – returns True if the TextCursor does not currently cover any highlighting.

14.6.2.   Formatting Text

The TextCursor service supports all of the character and paragraph properties that were described earlier in this chapter, so it is possible to format individual words of sentences. For example:

```
Dim oCursor As Object

oCursor = ThisComponent.createTextCursor

oCursor.gotoStartOfWord(False)
oCursor.gotoEndOfWord(True)
oCursor.CharWeight = com.sun.star.FontWeight.BOLD
```

The above example selects the current word and changes it to bold.

14.6.3.   Retrieving text content

By using the String property of a TextCursor, the currently highlighted area can be retrieved. For example:

```
Dim oCursor As Object

oCursor = ThisComponent.createTextCursor

oCursor.gotoStartOfWord(False)
oCursor.gotoEndOfWord(True)
MsgBox oCursor.String
```

This example selects the current word and outputs it in a message box.

14.6.4. Modifying text content

The String property can also be used to replace the current text or insert new text, by assigning a new value to the String property. If the cursor is currently highlighting text then that text will be replaced. If the cursor is not highlighting then the new text will be inserted at the current cursor position.

14.6.5. Searching for text content

It is also possible to search a text document for a particular phrase. This can be achieved using a SearchDescriptor. A SearchDescriptor is created using the createSearchDescriptor method of a document as follows:

```
Dim oSearchDesc As Object
oSearchDesc = ThisComponent.createSearchDescriptor
```

Once the SearchDescriptor is created you can then set the string to be searched for:

```
oSearchDesc.searchString = "Find me"
```

There are a number of additional properties that can be set that determine how the search works:

- SearchBackwards(Boolean) – searches backwards through the text.
- SearchCaseSensitive(Boolean) – toggles case sensitive searching on or off.
- SearchRegularExpression(Boolean) – treats the search string like a regular expression.
- SearchStyles(Boolean) – searches for a specified paragraph template.
- SearchWords(Boolean) – only searches for complete words.
- SearchSimilarity(Boolean) – performs a similarity search.
- SearchSimilarityAdd(Short) – number of chars which can be added for a similarity search.
- SearchSimilarityExchange(Short) – number of chars which can be replaced as part of similarity search.
- SearchSimilarityRemove(Short) – number of chars which can be removed as part of similarity search.
- SearchSimilarityRelax(Boolean) – consider all deviation rules at the same time for similarity search.

Once the SearchDescriptor has been set up it can be applied to the text document using the findFirst() and findNext() methods as follows:

```
Found = ThisComponent.findFirst(oSearchDesc)
Found = ThisComponent.findNext(Found.End, oSearchDesc)
```

The findFirst and findNext methods return a TextRange object referring to the found text.

14.6.6. Replacing text portions

In the same way that the searching for text is handled, so is replacing text within a document. The difference is that instead of using a SearchDescriptor, you use a ReplaceDescriptor. The ReplaceDescriptor supports all the properties previously described for the SearchDescriptor.

14.7. Non-text objects

Text documents contain more than just text paragraphs, they can also contain other objects such as tables and drawings. These objects can be anchored to any point within a text.

All of these objects support a common basic service called com.sun.star.TextContent, which provides the following properties:

- AnchorType(Enum) – determines the anchor type of a TextContent object.
- AnchorTypes(sequence of Enum) – enumeration of all AnchorTypes which support a special TextContent object.
- TextWrap(Enum) – determines the text wrap type around a TextContent object.

The TextContent objects also share methods for creating, inserting and deleting objects:

- createInstance – create a new TextContent object.
- insertTextContent – insert a TextContent object.
- removeTextContent – remove a TextContent object.

14.8. Creating a table

To create a table, a number of steps have to be taken:

1. An instance of a TextTable object is created.
2. The TextTable object it initialised with the number of rows and columns.
3. The TextTable is inserted at the current TextCursor position

The following code shows all of the above stages, creating a 3 row, 2 column table:

```
Dim oTable As Object
Dim oCursor As Object

Cursor = ThisComponent.createTextCursor()

oTable = ThisComponent.createInstance("com.sun.star.text.TextTable")
oTable.initialize(3, 2)

ThisComponent.Text.insertTextContent(oCursor, oTable, False)
```

The third argument of the insertTextContent method is a Boolean that indicates whether the table is to replace the current selection at the TextCursor (True) or be inserted before it (False).

An array containing references to all the TextTables in a text document can be obtained by using the getTextTables method of a Document object.

14.8.1.   Editing TextTables

OpenOffice.org Basic offers methods for accessing TextTables at table, row, column and cell level. The methods available depend on the level that is being operated on.

14.8.2. Table level

At table level, you can set properties that affect the formatting of the table. These are set using the com.sun.star.text.TextTable service and the following properties are available:

- BackColor(Long) – set the background colour of the table.
- BottomMargin(Long) – set the bottom margin in 100ths of a millimetre.
- LeftMargin(Long) – set the left margin in 100ths of a millimetre.
- RightMargin(Long) – set the right margin in 100ths of a millimetre.
- TopMargin(Long) – set the top margin in 100ths of a millimetre.
- RepeatHeadline(Boolean) – table header is repeated on every page.
- Width(Long) – the width of the table in 100ths of a millimetre.

14.8.3. Row level

Rows are accessed using the getRows() method of a table object, which returns a list of rows. The list of rows provides the following methods:

- getCount() – returns the number of row objects.
- getByIndex(Integer) – returns a row object for the specified index position.
- insertByIndex(Index, Count) – inserts Count rows in the table at the Index positon.
- removeByIndex(Index, Count) – removes Count rows from the table at the Index positon.

It should be noted that the insertByIndex and removeByIndex methods only work on tables that do not have merged cells.

Once you have obtained a Row object using the getByIndex method, you can set the following properties for it:

- BackColor(Long) – the background colour of the row.
- Height(Long) – the height of the row in 100ths of a Millimetre.
- IsAutoHeight(Boolean) – is the row height dynamically changed for the content.
- VertOrient(Const) – the vertical orientation of the text within the row.

14.8.4. Column level

Although columns are not strictly speaking provided in OpenOffice.org, Basic still provides methods for accessing them. However, no formatting can be undertaken at column level.

The getColumns() method of the table object is used to get a list of columns, then the getCount, getByIndex, insertByIndex and removeByIndex methods are available, as with row level.

14.8.5. Cell level

Cells are referenced in OpenOffice by a unique name, which has the format X# where X is a letter representing the column and # is the row number. The top left cell is 'A1'. It is possible to access a cell using the getCellByName() method of the table object.

A useful piece of code which will translate a row and column number into a cell name is:

```
cellName = Chr(Asc("A") – 1 + colNo) & rowNo
```

The getCellByName method returns a Cell object, which can have its content accessed/changed by the String property.

Cells also support the createTextCursor interface, which means that cells can be formatted using the methods associated with a TextCursor.

14.9. Inserting a text frame

Text Frames are created and inserted in the same way as tables, as described previously. An instance of com.sun.star.text.TextFrame is first created then this is inserted at a TextCursor location. TextFrames support the following main properties:

- AnchorType(const) – set the anchor type of the text frame.
- BackColor(Long) – set the background colour of the text frame.
- BottomMargin(Long) – set the bottom margin in 100ths of a millimetre.
- LeftMargin(Long) – set the left margin in 100ths of a millimetre.
- RightMargin(Long) – set the right margin in 100ths of a millimetre.
- TopMargin(Long) – set the top margin in 100ths of a millimetre.
- Height(Long) – set the height of text frame in 100ths of a millimetre.
- Width(Long) – set the width of text frame in 100ths of a millimetre.
- HoriOrient(const) – set the horizontal orientation of text frame.
- VertOrient(const) – set the vertical orientation of text frame.

TextFrames also support the TextCursor objects for editing/formatting the content of the TextFrame.

14.10. Inserting a text field

TextFields are used to insert information into a text document, such as the current date/time. The creation and insertion of a TextField follows exactly the same method as used for inserting TextTables and TextFrames. The only difference is that the instance that is created uses a sub-service of the com.sun.star.text.textfield service. The sub-services are described below for the different types of TextField.

14.10.1. Date/Time

To insert a date/time TextField create an instance of com.sun.star.text.textfield.DateTime to represent the current date or time. The resulting object will support the following properties:

- IsDate(Boolean) – if set to True, displays the current date, otherwise the time.
- IsFixed(Boolean) – if set to True then the time/date do not change, otherwise they are updated each time the document is opened.
- DateTimeValue(struct) – returns the current content of the object.
- NumberFormat(Const) – specifies the format that the time/date is displayed in.

14.10.2. Annotations

Annotation fields are comments that are placed against a particular piece of text. They can be created using com.sun.star.text.textfield.Annotation. The resulting object supports the following properties:

- Author(String) – the name of the author of the annotation.
- Content(String) – the text of the annotation.
- Date(Date) – the date that the annotation was written.

14.10.3. Chapter number / name

The number/name of the current chapter can be inserted using com.sun.star.text.textfield.Chapter. The resulting object supports the following properties:

- ChapterFormat(Const) – indicates whether chapter number or chapter name is displayed.
- Level(Int) – indicates the chapter level to be displayed.

14.10.4. Number of characters, words or pages

The number of characters, words and pages are inserted using the following:

- com.sun.star.text.textfield.CharacterCount for number of characters.
- com.sun.star.text.textfield.WordCount for number of words.
- com.sun.star.text.textfield.PageCount for number of pages.

All three support the NumberingType(Const) property which specifies the format of the numbering.

14.10.5. Current page number

The current page number can be inserted into the document using com.sun.star.text.textfield.PageNumber. The resulting object will support the following properties:

- NumberingType(Const) – the format of the number.
- Offset(Short) – positive or negative offset added to the page number.

14.11. Bookmarks

Book marks are TextContent objects and they are created using com.sun.star.text.Bookmark to create a Bookmark object and then assigning it a name using the Name property. The Bookmark is then inserted at the current TextCursor position.

Bookmarks can be accessed through a list in the Document object called Bookmarks. Individual Bookmarks are accessed either by number using the getByIndex() method or by name using the getByName method.

15. Spreadsheet Documents (Calc)

This chapter details how to interact with the services, methods and properties that relate to spreadsheet documents. First we will look at the structure of spreadsheet documents and how to access the individual elements of a spreadsheet document, then we will look at options for efficiently editing spreadsheets.

A spreadsheet document is formed of one or more spreadsheets (the tabs seen in the Calc front end). The document object of a spreadsheet document is based on the com.sun.star.sheet.SpreadsheetDocument service.

15.1. Spreadsheets

You can access the individual spreadsheets in a document using the Sheets list using either its name or number (starting at 0 for the first sheet) with the following code:

```
oSheet = ThisComponent.getSheets.getByIndex(0)
oSheet = ThisComponent.Sheets(0)
oSheet = ThisComponent.Sheets.getByName("Sheet 1")
```

The first 2 lines achieve the same thing, they return the first sheet. The third line returns the sheet named "Sheet 1" regardless of its position.

The Sheet object that is returned by the above methods supports the com.sun.star.sheet.Spreadsheet service and provides the following properties:

- IsVisible(Boolean) – True if the sheet is visible.
- PageStyle(String) – the name of the page template used for the sheet.

15.1.1. Renaming sheets

The Sheet object also supports the getName and setName methods to read and modify the name of the sheet. In Basic both methods can be used as a property Name, which both sets and gets the name of the sheet. The following code extract gets the first sheet's name and then renames it with "_old" appended:

```
Sheet = ThisComponent.Sheets(0)
oldName = Sheet.Name
Sheet.Name = oldName & "_old"
```

15.1.2. Creating and deleting sheets

The Sheets list of a spreadsheet document provides the methods for creating and deleting individual sheets. For creating sheets the process is to first check that a the sheet name does not already exist by using the hasByName() method. You then create an instance of a spreadsheet object using the createInstance method and finally use the insertByName method to create the sheet. This can be seen in action below:

```
Dim oSheet As Object

If (Not ThisComponent.Sheets.hasByName("New Sheet")) Then
    oSheet = ThisComponent.createInstance("com.sun.star.sheet.Spreadsheet")
    ThisComponent.Sheets.insertByName("New Sheet", oSheet)
End If
```

An alternative method of inserting a new sheet is to use the insertNewByName() method, which takes an additional Integer argument which specifies the position to insert the new sheet.

A method is also provided to remove a named sheet, using the removeByName() method. It is important though to first check that the sheet exists by using the hasByName() method, otherwise if you attempt to remove a non-existent sheet your code will error.

15.2. Rows and columns

Each sheet within a spreadsheet document contains a list of its rows and columns. These are available through the Rows and Columns properties of the spreadsheet object. The following code gets the first row and column objects:

```
Dim oSheet As Object
Dim oFirstRow As Object
Dim oFirstCol As Object

oSheet = ThisComponent.Sheets(0)

oFirstCol = oSheet.Columns(0)
oFirstRow = oSheet.Rows(0)
```

Column objects provide the following properties:

- Width(long) – the width of a column in hundredths of a millimeter.
- OptimalWidth(Boolean) - sets a column to its optimum width.
- IsVisible (Boolean) - displays a column.
- IsStartOfNewPage (Boolean) - when printing, creates a page break before a column.

Row objects provide the following similar properties:

- Height(long) – the height of a row in hundredths of a millimeter.
- OptimalHeight(Boolean) - sets a row to its optimum height.
- IsVisible (Boolean) - displays a row.
- IsStartOfNewPage (Boolean) - when printing, creates a page break before a row.

15.2.1.   Inserting and deleting rows and columns

The Rows and Columns objects both support insertByIndex() and removeByIndex() methods to insert and delete rows/columns. The syntax of the methods is shown in the following code:

```
Dim oSheet As Object

oSheet = ThisComponent.Sheets(0)

oSheet.Columns.insertByIndex(3, 1)
oSheet.Rows.insertByIndex(7, 2)

oSheet.Columns.removeByIndex(5, 2)
oSheet.Rows.removeByIndex(0, 1)
```

The arguments of the methods are the index (starting at 0) where the insertion/deletion is to take place and the number of rows/columns to insert or delete. So the above example first inserts a column into the 4th position and 2 rows into the 8th position. It then deletes 2 columns from the 6th position and the first row.

15.3.   Cells and ranges

In addition to recording the position of rows and columns, a spreadsheet object maintains a two-dimensional list of cells. Each cell is defined by its X and Y positions in relation to the top left cell which is at position (0, 0).

The Sheet object provides a means of accessing individual cells by using the getCellByPosition() method. The method takes two arguments, the X position and the Y position. The code below creates a Cell object that references the top left cell.

```
Dim oSheet As Object
Dim oCell As Object

oSheet = ThisComponent.Sheets(0)

oCell = oSheet.getCellByPosition(0, 0)
```

In addition to its numerical co-ordinates, each cell also has a name that corresponds to the column and row identifiers that appear in the Calc front-end. So the top left cell is known as 'A1'. The Sheet object provides an additional method for accessing a cell by name, the getCellRangeByName() method.

Whether you access a cell by position or by name, the returned Cell object is the same and has a number of properties for defining and obtaining the contents of the cell. In OpenOffice.org, a cell can be empty or contain text, numbers or formulas. The cell type is defined by the property that is used to populate it. The properties are as follows:

- Value – used to insert or obtain a number.
- String – used to insert or obtain text.
- Formula – used to insert or obtain a formula.

There is an additional property Type which will indicate the type of the contents of a cell. This property returns one of the following values:

- com.sun.star.table.CellContentType.EMPTY – the cell is empty.
- com.sun.star.table.CellContentType.VALUE – the cell contains a number.
- com.sun.star.table.CellContentType.TEXT – the cell contains a string.
- com.sun.star.table.CellContentType.FORMULA – the cell contains a formula.

15.3.1.   Inserting, deleting, moving and copying cells

The Spreadsheet object provides methods for inserting, deleting, moving and copying individual cells or ranges of cells. To use all of these methods, you first have to define a cell range structure. This is done as follows:

```
Dim CellRangeAddress As New com.sun.star.table.CellRangeAddress

CellRangeAddress.Sheet = 1
CellRangeAddress.StartColumn = 2
CellRangeAddress.StartRow = 1
CellRangeAddress.EndColumn = 5
CellRangeAddress.EndRow = 2
```

The above code defines a range on the second sheet that is 4 columns by 2 rows and starts at the 3rd column and 2nd row.

Once you have defined your range you can then insert or delete the range. Inserting cells is done using the insertCells() method, as seen in the code below:

```
oSheet.insertCells(CellRangeAddress, com.sun.star.sheet.CellInsertMode.DOWN)
```

The second parameter indicates what is done with the values that are in front of the insert point. This can have the following values:

- com.sun.star.sheet.CellInsertMode.NONE – the current values remain in their present position.
- com.sun.star.sheet.CellInsertMode.DOWN – the cells at and under the insert position are moved downwards.
- com.sun.star.sheet.CellInsertMode.RIGHT – the cells at and to the right of the insert position are moved to the right.
- com.sun.star.sheet.CellInsertMode.ROWS – the rows after the insert position are moved downwards.
- com.sun.star.sheet.CellInsertMode.COLUMNS – the columns after the insert position are moved to the right.

The removeRange() method is used to delete the range of cells. Its syntax is:

```
oSheet.removeRange(CellRangeAddress, com.sun.star.sheet.CellDeleteMode.UP)
```

The second parameter indicates what is done with the values that are behind the delete point. This can have the following values:

- com.sun.star.sheet.CellDeleteMode.NONE – the current values remain in their present position.
- com.sun.star.sheet.CellDeleteMode.UP – the cells at and below the delete position are moved upwards.
- com.sun.star.sheet.CellDeleteMode.LEFT – the cells at and to the right of the delete position are moved to the left.
- com.sun.star.sheet.CellDeleteMode.ROWS – the rows after the delete position are moved upwards.
- com.sun.star.sheet.CellDeleteMode.COLUMNS – the columns after the delete position are moved to the left.

The moving and copying of cells works in broadly the same way, except that there is an additional structure to be defined which holds the position of the destination. This is created as follows:

```
Dim CellAddress As New com.sun.star.table.CellAddress

CellAddress.Sheet = 0
CellAddress.Column = 1
CellAddress.Row = 2
```

The above code defines the destination as cell B3 of the first sheet.

Once the source range and destination address have been defined you can use the moveRange() and copyRange() methods to move or copy the cells. These have the following syntax:

```
oSheet.moveRange(CellAddress, CellRangeAddress)

oSheet.copyRange(CellAddress, CellRangeAddress)
```

15.4. Formatting cells

In addition to supporting the CharacterProperties and ParagraphProperties services, Cell objects also support the com.sun.star.table.CellProperties service, which provides cell specific formatting properties.

15.4.1. Background colours

Two properties are provided for the definition of background colours:

- CellBackColor(Long) – defines the background colour of the cell.
- IsCellBackgroundTransparent(Boolean) – sets the background colour to transparent.

15.4.2. Shadows

Cells can also have shadows applied to them using the ShadowFormat property. This takes as its argument a com.sun.star.table.ShadowFormat structure, which has the following properties:

- Location(enum) – the position of shadow (value from the com.sun.star.table.ShadowLocation structure).
- ShadowWidth(Short) – the size of shadow in hundredths of a millimetre.
- IsTransparent(Boolean) – sets the shadow to transparent.
- Color(Long) – sets the colour of shadow

The following code sets the shadow of a cell to 2mm in a red colour:

```
Dim ShadowFormat As New com.sun.star.table.ShadowFormat

ShadowFormat.Location = com.sun.star.table.ShadowLocation.BOTTOM_RIGHT
ShadowFormat.ShadowWidth = 200
ShadowFormat.Color = RGB(255, 0, 0)

oCell.ShadowFormat = ShadowFormat
```

15.4.3. Text justification

A number of properties are also provided to change the justification of text within a cell.

- HoriJustify(enum) – horizontal justification of the text (value from com.sun.star.table.CellHoriJustify).
- VertJustify(enum) – vertical justification of the text (value from com.sun.star.table.CellVertJustify).
- Orientation(enum) – orientation of text (value in accordance with com.sun.star.table.CellOrientation).
- IsTextWrapped(Boolean) – permits automatic line breaks within the cell.
- RotateAngle(Long) – angle of rotation of text in hundredths of a degree.

15.4.4. Date, number and text formats

There are a whole range of predefined formats for formatting the contents of a cell. These can be seen by using the **Format Cells** dialog in Calc. The format of a cell can be changed using the NumberFormat property. The available formats are accessed through the NumberFormats object of the Document. This object provides two methods for accessing existing formats and creating new ones:

- queryKey() – identifies an existing format based on a format string.
- addNew() – adds a new format to the document.

The code below formats cell A1 so that numbers are displayed to two decimal places and with a comma as a thousands separator:

```
Dim oSheet As Object
Dim oCell As Object
Dim oNumberFormats As Object
Dim NumberFormatString As String
Dim NumberFormatId As Long
Dim LocalSettings As New com.sun.star.lang.Locale

oSheet = ThisComponent.Sheets(0)
oCell = oSheet.getCellByPosition(1,1)

oCell.Value = 123456.789876

LocalSettings.Language = "en"
LocalSettings.Country = "us"

oNumberFormats = ThisComponent.NumberFormats
NumberFormatString = "#,##0.00"

NumberFormatId = oNumberFormats.queryKey(NumberFormatString, LocalSettings, True)
```

```
If NumberFormatId = -1 Then
    NumberFormatId = oNumberFormats.addNew(NumberFormatString, Local§Settings)
End If

oCell.NumberFormat = NumberFormatId
```

15.5. Page properties

Page properties are options that provide visual elements that are repeated on a number of pages and also the positioning of a document on the page. They include:

- Margins
- Paper formats
- Headers and footers

Page properties are defined by applying them to a page style and then using that page style in the document.

The following sections describe the page properties that are available for spreadsheet documents.

15.5.1. Page background properties

The following properties are available for defining the background of a page:

- BackColor(Long) – defines the colour of the background.
- BackGraphicURL(String) – defines the URL of the graphic to be used for the background.
- BackGraphicFilter(String) – defines the name of the filter for interpreting the background graphics.
- BackGraphicLocation(Enum) – defines the position of the background.
- BackTransparent(Boolean) – defines whether the background is transparent.

15.5.2. Paper format properties

The following properties are available for defining the paper format used by the page:

- IsLandscape(Boolean) – makes the page landscape format.
- Width(Long) – defines the width of the page in hundredths of a millimetre.
- Height(Long) – defines the length of the page in hundredths of a millimetre.
- PrinterPaperTray(String) – defines the name of the printer paper tray to use.

15.5.3. Page margins, borders and shadows

The setting of page margins, borders and shadows can be achieved using the following properties:

- LeftMargin(long) – width of the left hand page margin in hundredths of a millimetre.
- RightMargin(long) – width of the right hand page margin in hundredths of a millimetre.
- TopMargin(long) – width of the top page margin in hundredths of a millimetre.
- BottomMargin(long) – width of the bottom page margin in hundredths of a millimetre.
- LeftBorder(struct) – specifications for left-hand line of page border.
- RightBorder(struct) – specifications for right-hand line of page border.
- TopBorder(struct) – specifications for top line of page border.
- BottomBorder(struct) – specifications for bottom line of page border.
- LeftBorderDistance(long) – distance between left-hand page border and page content in hundredths of a millimetre.
- RightBorderDistance(long) – distance between right-hand page border and page content in hundredths of a millimetre.
- TopBorderDistance(long) – distance between top page border and page content in hundredths of a millimetre.
- BottomBorderDistance(long) – distance between bottom page border and page content in hundredths of a millimetre.
- ShadowFormat(struct) – specifications for shadow of content area of page.

15.5.4.   Headers and footers

The headers and footers of a document can also be set using the following properties. To set the header:

- HeaderIsOn(Boolean) – header is activated.
- HeaderLeftMargin(long) – distance between header and left-hand page margin in hundredths of a millimetre.
- HeaderRightMargin(long) – distance between header and right-hand page margin in hundredths of a millimetre.
- HeaderBodyDistance(long) – distance between header and main body of document in hundredths of a millimetre.
- HeaderHeight(long) – height of header in hundredths of a millimetre.
- HeaderIsDynamicHeight(Boolean) – height of header is automatically adapted to content.
- HeaderLeftBorder(struct) – details of the left-hand border of frame around header.
- HeaderRightBorder(struct) – details of the right-hand border of frame around header.
- HeaderTopBorder(struct) – details of the top line of the border around header.
- HeaderBottomBorder(struct) – details of the bottom line of the border around header.
- HeaderLeftBorderDistance(long) – distance between left-hand border and content of header in hundredths of a millimetre.
- HeaderRightBorderDistance(long) – distance between right-hand border and content of header in hundredths of a millimetre.
- HeaderTopBorderDistance(long) – distance between top border and content of header in hundredths of a millimetre.
- HeaderBottomBorderDistance(long) – distance between bottom border and content of header in hundredths of a millimetre.
- HeaderIsShared(Boolean) – headers on even and odd pages have the same content.
- HeaderBackColor(long) – background color of header.
- HeaderBackGraphicURL(String) – URL of the background graphics that you want to use.
- HeaderBackGraphicFilter(String) – name of the filter for interpreting the background graphics for the header.

- HeaderBackGraphicLocation(Enum) – position of the background graphics for the header.
- HeaderBackTransparent(Boolean) – shows the background of the header as transparent.
- HeaderShadowFormat(struct) – details of shadow of header.

For working with the footer, there are a set of similarly named functions (just replace Header with Footer in the name).

15.5.5. Changing header and footer text

The textual content of headers and footers is available through the following properties:

- LeftPageHeaderContent(Object) – content of headers for even pages.
- RightPageHeaderContent(Object) – content of headers for odd pages.
- LeftPageFooterContent(Object) – content of footers for even pages.
- RightPageFooterContent(Object) – content of footers for odd pages.

If you have set the HeaderIsShared/FooterIsShared property to true, then you only need to worry about setting the properties for odd pages.

All the objects that are returned/passed support the com.sun.star.sheet.HeaderFooterContent service. This service provides three properties LeftText, CenterText and RightText to set three elements for the headers and footers.

The example below writes "OpenOfficeBasic – An Introduction" in the center text field of the default template header.

```
Dim StyleFamilies As Object
Dim PageStyles As Object
Dim DefPage As Object
Dim HText As Object
Dim HContent As Object

StyleFamilies = ThisComponent.StyleFamilies
PageStyles = StyleFamilies.getByName("PageStyles")
DefPage = PageStyles.getByName("Default")

DefPage.HeaderIsOn = True
DefPage.HeaderIsShared = True
HContent = DefPage.RightPageHeaderContent
HText = HContent.CenterText
HText.String = "OpenOfficeBasic – An Introduction"
DefPage.RightPageHeaderContent = HContent
```

15.5.6. Printing spreadsheets

The com.sun.star.sheet.TablePageStyle service provides a number of properties that define how your spreadsheet will look when it is printed. These are as follows:

- CenterHorizontally(Boolean) – table content is centered horizontally.
- CenterVertically(Boolean) – table content is centered vertically.
- PrintAnnotations(Boolean) – prints cell comments.
- PrintGrid(Boolean) – prints the cell gridlines.
- PrintHeaders(Boolean) – prints the row and column headings.
- PrintCharts(Boolean) – prints charts contained in a sheet.
- PrintObjects(Boolean) – prints embedded objects.
- PrintDrawing(Boolean) – prints draw objects.
- PrintDownFirst(Boolean) – if the contents of a sheet extend across several pages, they are first printed in vertically descending order, and then down the right-hand side.
- PrintFormulas(Boolean) – prints the formulas instead of the calculated values.
- PrintZeroValues(Boolean) – prints the zero values.

16. Drawing documents (Draw)

This chapter deals with the interaction with Draw documents available with OpenOffice.org Basic.

16.1. Document structure – pages

A Draw document is composed of pages, as are Impress presentations. There is no limit to the number of pages in a drawing document and each page can be designed separately. There is also no limit to the number of elements that you can have on each page.

Pages are available through the DrawPages method and can be accessed either by number or name, in the same way as spreadsheets in a Calc document are accessed. The following code examples show the two methods:

```
Page = ThisComponent.DrawPages(0)
Page = ThisComponent.DrawPages.getByName("Page 1")
```

16.1.1. Page properties

The object that is returned by the DrawPages methods supports the com.sun.star.drawing.DrawPage service, which has the following properties:

- BorderLeft(Long) – left-hand border in hundredths of a millimetre.
- BorderRight(Long) – right-hand border in hundredths of a millimetre.
- BorderTop(Long) – top border in hundredths of a millimetre.
- BorderBottom(Long) – bottom border in hundredths of a millimetre.
- Width(Long) – page width in hundredths of a millimetre.
- Height(Long) – page height in hundredths of a millimetre.
- Number(Short) – number of pages (read-only).
- Orientation(Enum) – page orientation.

Changing these settings will affect **all** pages in a document.

16.1.2. Renaming pages

Pages provide the getName and setName methods to read and modify the page's name. In Basic, the Name property can also be used to both get and set the name. In the following example, we rename the first page of a drawing document:

```
Dim Page As Object

Page = ThisComponent.DrawPages(0)
Page.Name = "First"
```

16.1.3. Inserting and deleting pages

The DrawPages object is also used for inserting and deleting individual pages. Before attempting to insert or delete a page, it is important to check whether it already exists. Three methods are provided:

- hasByName(String) – check to see whether the page exists.
- insertByIndex(Int) – insert a new page after the index number given (starting from 0).
- remove(obj) – remove the page that is referenced.

16.1.4. Copying a page

Copy pages are created using the duplicate method, which is provided by the document object. The copy page is inserted at the position after the original page, with a default name. The following example copies a page and then renames it:

```
Dim Page As Object
Dim ClonedPage As Object

Page = ThisComponent.Drawpages.getByName("MyPage")
ClonedPage = ThisComponent.duplicate(Page)
ClonedPage.Name = "MyCopy"
```

16.2. Drawing object properties

Drawings are made up of a number of drawing objects (such as circles and rectangles), which all have properties that can be worked with.

16.2.1. Common properties

A number of the properties are common across all shapes, these include the Size and Position properties. The following code example creates a rectangle and positions it in the document:

```
Dim Page As Object
Dim RectangleShape As Object
Dim Point As New com.sun.star.awt.Point
Dim Size As New com.sun.star.awt.Size

Page = ThisComponent.DrawPages(0)

Point.x = 1000
Point.y = 1000
Size.Width = 10000
Size.Height = 10000

RectangleShape = ThisComponent.createInstance("com.sun.star.drawing.RectangleShape")
RectangleShape.Size = Size
RectangleShape.Position = Point

Page.add(RectangleShape)
```

The code first defines Point and Size structures and defines them with values in hundredths of a millimetre. The code then creates an instance of a RectangleShape and sets the shape's size and position. Finally, the code uses the add method to add the shape to the page.

16.2.2. Fill properties

Draw provides a number of different types of fill options, which can be accessed through Basic. The type of fill that is being used is defined using the FillStyle property.

Single colour fills

The simplest type of fill is the single colour fill. This uses a FillStyle mode of SOLID and uses one property FillColor, which defines the colour of the fill. The following code creates a rectangle and fills it with green:

```
Dim Page As Object
Dim RectangleShape As Object
Dim Point As New com.sun.star.awt.Point
Dim Size As New com.sun.star.awt.Size

Point.x = 1000
Point.y = 1000
Size.Width = 10000
Size.Height = 10000

Page = ThisComponent.DrawPages(0)

RectangleShape = ThisComponent.createInstance("com.sun.star.drawing.RectangleShape")
RectangleShape.Size = Size
RectangleShape.Position = Point

RectangleShape.FillStyle = com.sun.star.drawing.FillStyle.SOLID
RectangleShape.FillColor = RGB(255, 0, 0)

Page.add(RectangleShape)
```

Colour gradients

The second type of fill is a colour gradient, which is set using a FillStyle of GRADIENT. To define a colour gradient you have to use a com.sun.star.awt.Gradient structure, which is assigned to the FillGradient property. The following properties are available for defining the gradient:

- Style(Enum) – type of gradient, for example, linear or radial.
- StartColor(Long) – start color of color gradient.
- EndColor(Long) – end color of color gradient.
- Angle(Short) – angle of color gradient in tenths of a degree.
- XOffset(Short) – X-coordinate at which the color gradient starts, specified in hundredths of a millimetre.
- YOffset(Short) – Y-coordinate at which the color gradient begins, specified in hundredths of a millimetre.

- StartIntensity(Short) – intensity of StartColor as a percentage.
- EndIntensity(Short) – intensity of EndColor as a percentage.
- StepCount(Short) – number of color graduations which OpenOffice.org is to calculate for the gradients.

The following code example defines a gradient that goes from black to white:

```
Dim Page As Object
Dim RectangleShape As Object
Dim Point As New com.sun.star.awt.Point
Dim Size As New com.sun.star.awt.Size
Dim Gradient As New com.sun.star.awt.Gradient

Point.x = 1000
Point.y = 1000
Size.Width = 10000
Size.Height = 10000

Page = ThisComponent.DrawPages(0)

RectangleShape = ThisComponent.createInstance("com.sun.star.drawing.RectangleShape")
RectangleShape.Size = Size
RectangleShape.Position = Point
Gradient.Style = com.sun.star.awt.GradientStyle.LINEAR
Gradient.StartColor = RGB(0, 0, 0)
Gradient.EndColor = RGB(255, 255, 255)
Gradient.StartIntensity = 100
Gradient.EndIntensity = 100
Gradient.Angle = 450
Gradient.StepCount = 100

RectangleShape.FillStyle = com.sun.star.drawing.FillStyle.GRADIENT
RectangleShape.FillGradient = Gradient

Page.add(RectangleShape)
```

Hatching

The third type of fill is a hatch fill, which is created by specifying a FillStyle propery of HATCH. A com.sun.star.drawing.Hatch structure has to be defined, which has the following properties:

- Style(Enum) – type of hatch: simple, squared, or squared with diagonals.
- Color(Long) – color of lines.
- Distance(Long) – distance between lines in hundredths of a millimetre.
- Angle(Short) – angle of hatch in tenths of a degree.

The code below demonstrates the use of a simple hatch structure in a rectangle object:

```
Dim Page As Object
Dim RectangleShape As Object
Dim Point As New com.sun.star.awt.Point
Dim Size As New com.sun.star.awt.Size
Dim Hatch As New com.sun.star.drawing.Hatch

Point.x = 1000
Point.y = 1000
Size.Width = 10000
Size.Height = 10000

Page = ThisComponent.DrawPages(0)

RectangleShape = ThisComponent.createInstance("com.sun.star.drawing.RectangleShape")
RectangleShape.Size = Size
RectangleShape.Position = Point

RectangleShape.FillStyle = com.sun.star.drawing.FillStyle.HATCH

Hatch.Style = com.sun.star.drawing.HatchStyle.SINGLE
Hatch.Color = RGB(255, 0, 0)
Hatch.Distance = 30
Hatch.Angle = 450

RectangleShape.FillHatch = Hatch

Page.add(RectangleShape)
```

Bitmap fill

The final type of fill is the bitmap, which is achieved using a FillStyle of BITMAP. The bitmap can either be one of the predefined ones that is available in OpenOffice.org, or you can load your own. If the bitmap is already available then you just use its name in the FillBitmapName property, otherwise you must specify the location of the external file using the FillBitmapURL property. The following code creates a rectangle and fills it with the Water bitmap that is available:

```
Dim Page As Object
Dim RectangleShape As Object
Dim Point As New com.sun.star.awt.Point
Dim Size As New com.sun.star.awt.Size

Point.x = 1000
Point.y = 1000
Size.Width = 10000
Size.Height = 10000

Page = ThisComponent.DrawPages(0)

RectangleShape = ThisComponent.createInstance("com.sun.star.drawing.RectangleShape")
RectangleShape.Size = Size
RectangleShape.Position = Point

RectangleShape.FillStyle = com.sun.star.drawing.FillStyle.BITMAP
RectangleShape.FillBitmapName = "Water"
RectangleShape.FillBitmapMode = com.sun.star.drawing.BitmapMode.REPEAT

Page.add(RectangleShape)
```

Fill transparency

Whichever one of the four fill types you are using, you can change the transparency level of the fill by using the FillTransparence property. It is also possible to use the FillTransparenceGradient property to define a gradient that specifies the transparency of the fill area.

16.2.3. Line properties

Drawing objects that can have a border support the com.sun.star.drawing.LineStyle service, which is used to define the border. Some of the properties provided by this service include:

- LineStyle(Enum) – defines the line type (solid, dashed, dotted etc).
- LineColor(Long) – defines the line color.
- LineTransparence(Short) – defines the line transparency.
- LineWidth(Long) – the line thickness in hundredths of a millimetre.
- LineJoint(Enum) – defines transitions to connection points.

The code example below creates a rectangle with a solid 10 millimetre mitred cornered border:

```
Dim Page As Object
Dim RectangleShape As Object
Dim Point As New com.sun.star.awt.Point
Dim Size As New com.sun.star.awt.Size

Point.x = 1000
Point.y = 1000
Size.Width = 10000
Size.Height = 10000

Page = ThisComponent.DrawPages(0)

RectangleShape = ThisComponent.createInstance("com.sun.star.drawing.RectangleShape")
RectangleShape.Size = Size
RectangleShape.Position = Point

RectangleShape.LineColor = RGB(128, 128, 128)
RectangleShape.LineTransparence = 50
RectangleShape.LineWidth = 1000
RectangleShape.LineJoint = com.sun.star.drawing.LineJoint.MITER
RectangleShape.LineStyle = com.sun.star.drawing.LineStyle.SOLID

Page.add(RectangleShape)
```

16.2.4. Text properties

Text in drawing objects is formatted using the CharacterProperties and ParagraphProperties services that were described in the chapter relating to text documents.

The text is inserted into the drawing object after it has been added to the page, using the String property of the shape.

The text can be positioned and formatted using the com.sun.star.drawing.Text service, which provides the following properties:

- TextAutoGrowHeight(Boolean) – adapts the height of the drawing element to the text it contains.
- TextAutoGrowWidth(Boolean) – adapts the width of the drawing element to the text it contains.
- TextHorizontalAdjust(Enum) – horizontal position of text within the drawing element.
- TextVerticalAdjust(Enum) – vertical position of text within the drawing element.
- TextLeftDistance(Long) – left-hand distance between drawing element and text in hundredths of a millimetre.
- TextRightDistance(Long) – right-hand distance between drawing element and text in hundredths of a millimetre.
- TextUpperDistance(Long) – upper distance between drawing element and text in hundredths of a millimetre.
- TextLowerDistance(Long) – lower distance between drawing element and text in hundredths of a millimetre.

16.2.5. Shadow properties

Most drawing objects can have a shadow applied to them using the com.sun.star.drawing.ShadowProperties service, which has the following properties:

- Shadow(Boolean) – activates the shadow.
- ShadowColor(Long) – shadow colour.
- ShadowTransparence(Short) – transparency of the shadow.
- ShadowXDistance(Long) – vertical distance of the shadow from the drawing object in hundredths of a millimetre.
- ShadowYDistance(Long) – horizontal distance of the shadow from the drawing object in hundredths of a millimetre.

16.3. Different drawing objects

The following are the different drawing objects that are provided and an overview of the properties available for formatting them.

16.3.1. Rectangle shapes

Rectangle objects (com.sun.star.drawing.RectangleShape), support the following services and their properties for formatting:

- Fill properties – com.sun.star.drawing.FillProperties.
- Line properties – com.sun.star.drawing.LineProperties.
- Text properties – com.sun.star.drawing.Text.
- Shadow properties – com.sun.star.drawing.ShadowProperties.

Additionally, rectangles support the following property:

- CornerRadius(Long) – radius for rounding corners in hundredths of a millimetre.

16.3.2. Circles and ellipses

Circle and ellipse objects (com.sun.star.drawing.EllipseShape), support the following services and their properties for formatting:

- Fill properties – com.sun.star.drawing.FillProperties.
- Line properties – com.sun.star.drawing.LineProperties.
- Text properties – com.sun.star.drawing.Text.
- Shadow properties – com.sun.star.drawing.ShadowProperties.

Additionally, circles and ellipses support the following property:

- CircleKind(Enum) – type of circle or ellipse.
- CircleStartAngle(Long) – start angle in tenths of a degree (only for circle or ellipse segments)
- CircleEndAngle(Long) – end angle in tenths of a degree (only for circle or ellipse segments)

The CircleKind property indicates whether the object is a whole circle a slice of a section. It takes the following values:

- com.sun.star.drawing.CircleKind.FULL – full circle or full ellipse.
- com.sun.star.drawing.CircleKind.CUT – section of circle (partial circle whose interfaces are linked directly to one another).
- com.sun.star.drawing.CircleKind.SECTION – circle slice.
- com.sun.star.drawing.CircleKind.ARC – angle (not including circle line).

The example below creates a circular slice with a 45 degree angle:

```
Dim Page As Object
Dim EllipseShape As Object
Dim Point As New com.sun.star.awt.Point
Dim Size As New com.sun.star.awt.Size

Point.x = 1000
Point.y = 1000
Size.Width = 10000
Size.Height = 10000

Page = ThisComponent.DrawPages(0)

EllipseShape = ThisComponent.createInstance("com.sun.star.drawing.EllipseShape")
EllipseShape.Size = Size
EllipseShape.Position = Point

EllipseShape.CircleStartAngle = 3000
EllipseShape.CircleEndAngle = 7500
EllipseShape.CircleKind =  com.sun.star.drawing.CircleKind.SECTION

Page.add(EllipseShape)
```

16.3.3.   Line objects

Line objects are provided by the com.sun.star.drawing.LineShape service, which supports the following properties:

- Line properties – com.sun.star.drawing.LineProperties.
- Text properties – com.sun.star.drawing.Text.
- Shadow properties – com.sun.star.drawing.ShadowProperties.

16.3.4. Polypolygon shapes

Complex polygonal shapes are supported through the com.sun.star.drawing.PolyPolygonShape service. The service supports all the standard properties:

- Fill properties – com.sun.star.drawing.FillProperties.
- Line properties – com.sun.star.drawing.LineProperties.
- Text properties – com.sun.star.drawing.Text.
- Shadow properties – com.sun.star.drawing.ShadowProperties.

In addition, the PolyPolygon(Array) property is provided, which allows for the definition of the coordinates of the polygon. The following example creates a triangle:

```
Dim Page As Object
Dim PolyPolygonShape As Object
Dim PolyPolygon As Variant
Dim Coordinates(2) As New com.sun.star.awt.Point

Page = ThisComponent.DrawPages(0)

PolyPolygonShape = ThisComponent.createInstance("com.sun.star.drawing.PolyPolygonShape")
Page.add(PolyPolygonShape)    ' Page.add must take place before the coordinates are set

Coordinates(0).x = 1000
Coordinates(1).x = 7500
Coordinates(2).x = 10000
Coordinates(0).y = 1000
Coordinates(1).y = 7500
Coordinates(2).y = 5000

PolyPolygonShape.PolyPolygon = Array(Coordinates())
```

As the polygon is defined by coordinates, there is no need to define its position or its size.

16.3.5. Graphics

The final drawing element is the graphics object, which are based on the com.sun.star.drawing.GraphicObjectShape and can be used with any graphic or image.

Graphic objects support two of the general formatting properties:

- Text properties – com.sun.star.drawing.Text.
- Shadow properties – com.sun.star.drawing.ShadowProperties.

Additionally, the following specific properties are supported:

- GraphicURL(String) – URL of the graphic.
- AdjustLuminance(Short) – luminance of the colours, as a percentage (negative values are also permitted).
- AdjustContrast(Short) – contrast as a percentage (negative values are also permitted).
- AdjustRed(Short) – red value as a percentage (negative values are also permitted).
- AdjustGreen(Short) – green value as a percentage (negative values are also permitted).
- AdjustBlue(Short) – blue value as a percentage (negative values are also permitted).
- Gamma(Short) – gamma value of a graphic.
- Transparency(Short) – transparency of a graphic as a percentage.
- GraphicColorMode(enum) – colour mode, for example, standard, grey stages, black and white.

16.4. Editing drawing objects

16.4.1. Grouping objects

Draw offers the facility for you to group objects together and then edit that group. This is achieved by creating an object that supports the com.sun.star.drawing.ShapeCollection service and adding the individual objects to that object. The ShapeCollection is added to the page using the group method which returns the Group object, which can then be edited like an individual shape. The code below creates two objects, groups them and then centres them on the page:

```
Dim Page As Object
Dim Square As Object
Dim Circle As Object
Dim Shapes As Object
Dim Group As Object
Dim Point As New com.sun.star.awt.Point
Dim Size As New com.sun.star.awt.Size
Dim NewPos As New com.sun.star.awt.Point
Dim Height As Long
Dim Width As Long

Page = ThisComponent.DrawPages(0)
Point.x = 3000
Point.y = 3000
Size.Width = 3000
Size.Height = 3000

' create square drawing element
Square = ThisComponent.createInstance("com.sun.star.drawing.RectangleShape")
Square.Size = Size
Square.Position = Point
Square.FillColor = RGB(255, 128, 128)
Page.add(Square)

' create circle drawing element
Circle = ThisComponent.createInstance("com.sun.star.drawing.EllipseShape")
Circle.Size = Size
Circle.Position = Point
Circle.FillColor = RGB(0, 255, 0)
Page.add(Circle)

' combine square and circle drawing elements
Shapes = createUnoService("com.sun.star.drawing.ShapeCollection")
Shapes.add(Square)
Shapes.add(Circle)
Group = Page.group(Shapes)
```

```
' centre combined drawing elements
Height = Page.Height
Width = Page.Width
NewPos.X = Width / 2
NewPos.Y = Height / 2
Height = Group.Size.Height
Width = Group.Size.Width
NewPos.X = NewPos.X - Width / 2
NewPos.Y = NewPos.Y - Height / 2
Group.Position = NewPos
```

16.4.2. Rotating and shearing drawing objects

The objects that have been described in the previous sections can all be rotated or sheared by using the com.sun.star.drawing.RotationDescriptor service. This service provides the following properties:

- RotateAngle(Long) – rotary angle in hundredths of a degree
- ShearAngle(Long) – shear angle in hundredths of a degree

The following example creates a square and rotates it through 45 degrees.

```
Dim Page As Object
Dim RectangleShape As Object
Dim Point As New com.sun.star.awt.Point
Dim Size As New com.sun.star.awt.Size

Point.x = 1000
Point.y = 1000
Size.Width = 5000
Size.Height = 5000

Page = ThisComponent.DrawPages(0)

RectangleShape = ThisComponent.createInstance("com.sun.star.drawing.RectangleShape")
RectangleShape.Size = Size
RectangleShape.Position = Point

RectangleShape.RotateAngle = 4500

Page.add(RectangleShape)
```

16.4.3. Searching and replacing

It is possible to search and replace text within drawing documents. This is done using the createReplacementDescriptor method of a Page object to define the text to be replaced and then use the ReplaceAll method to actually make the replacement. The following example replaces text in all pages in a document:

```
Dim Page As Object
Dim ReplaceDescriptor As Object
Dim I As Integer

Page = ThisComponent.DrawPages(0)

ReplaceDescriptor = Page.createReplaceDescriptor()
ReplaceDescriptor.SearchString = "he"
ReplaceDescriptor.ReplaceString = "she"

For I = 0 to ThisComponent.DrawPages.Count - 1
    Page = ThisComponent.DrawPages(I)
    Page.ReplaceAll(ReplaceDescriptor)
Next I
```

17. Presentation documents (Impress)

OpenOffice.opg's presentation software is Impress and its documents are based on drawing documents, with each page in the document being a slide. The objects within a presentation document are worked with in the same way as drawing documents described in the previous chapter. There are however additional functions that are provided by the com.sun.star.presentation.PresentationDocument service.

17.1. Working with presentations

The Presentation object is provided to allow interaction with the main properties and functions of presentation documents. The presentation object provides the following three methods:

- Start – starts the presentation.
- End – ends the presentation.
- rehearseTimings – starts the presentation from the beginning and establishes its runtime.

The service also provides the following properties:

- AllowAnimations(Boolean) – runs animations in the presentation.
- CustomShow(String) – allows you to specify the name of the presentation so that you can reference the name in the presentation.
- FirstPage(String) – name of slide that you want to start the presentation with.
- IsAlwaysOnTop(Boolean) – always displays the presentation window as the first window on the screen.
- IsAutomatic(Boolean) – automatically runs through the presentation.
- IsEndless(Boolean) – restarts the presentation from the beginning once it ends.
- IsFullScreen(Boolean) – automatically starts the presentation in full screen mode.
- IsMouseVisible(Boolean) – displays the mouse during the presentation.
- Pause(long) – the amount of time that a blank screen is displayed at the end of the presentation.
- StartWithNavigator(Boolean) – displays the navigator window when the presentation starts.
- UsePn(Boolean) – displays the pointer during the presentation.

The following code sets a presentation to run in full screen mode in an endless loop and then starts the presentation.

```
Dim Presentation As Object

Presentation = ThisComponent.Presentation

Presentation.IsAutomatic = True
Presentation.IsFullScreen = True

Presentation.start()
```

18. Charts

Charts within OpenOffice.org are not treated as individual document types, but as objects that can be inserted in to other documents (for example spreadsheets). There are a number of different types of chart that can be displayed, such as pie charts, line graphs and bar charts.

Charts can be set up so that they contain their own data or they can display data from the document they are contained in (for example data from cell ranges in a spreadsheet).

18.1. Charts in spreadsheets

As mentioned above, charts in spreadsheets take their data from a defined cell range, so when the chart is created the range must be passed as one of the arguments.

The following code creates a bar chart based on data from cells A1 to C10 in the first sheet of the document

```
Dim Charts As Object
Dim Rect As New com.sun.star.awt.Rectangle
Dim RangeAddress(0) As New com.sun.star.table.CellRangeAddress

Charts = ThisComponent.Sheets(0).Charts

Rect.X = 8000
Rect.Y = 1000
Rect.Width = 10000
Rect.Height = 7000
RangeAddress(0).Sheet = 0
RangeAddress(0).StartColumn = 0
RangeAddress(0).StartRow = 0
RangeAddress(0).EndColumn = 2
RangeAddress(0).EndRow = 9

Charts.addNewByName("MyChart", Rect, RangeAddress(), True, True)
```

18.2. Types of chart

OpenOffice.org provides a number of different chart types, which have different properties associated with them.

18.2.1. Line charts

Line charts are supported by the com.sun.star.chart.LineDiagram service. They can be displayed in either 2D or 3D format, using the com.sun.star.chart.Dim3Ddiagram service. They are also stackable, using the com.sun.star.chart.StackableDiagram service.

Line charts provide the following properties:

- SymbolType(const) – symbol for displaying the data points.
- SymbolBitmapURL(String) – file name of graphics for displaying the data points.
- Lines(Boolean) – links the data points by means of lines.
- SplineType(Long) – spline function for smoothing the lines (0: no spline function, 1: cubic splines, 2: B splines).
- SplineOrder(Long) – polynomial weight for splines (only for B splines).
- SplineResolution(Long) – number of support points for spline calculation.

18.2.2. Area charts

Area charts are supported by the com.sun.star.chart.AreaDiagram service and are also available in 2D or 3D and stackable. The AreaDiagram service does not provide any properties of its own.

18.2.3. Bar charts

Bar charts are supported by the com.sun.star.chart.BarDiagram service. They are also available in 2D or 3D and are stackable. The following properties are provided:

- Vertical(Boolean) – displays the bars vertically, otherwise they are depicted horizontally.
- Deep(Boolean) – in 3D viewing mode, positions the bars behind one another rather than next to one another.
- StackedBarsConnected(Boolean) – links the associated bars in a stacked chart by means of lines (only available with horizontal charts).
- GroupBarsPerAxis(Boolean) – displays bars attached to different axes behind or next to each other.

18.2.4. Pie charts

Pie charts are supported by the com.sun.star.chart.PieDiagram service. They can be either 2D or 3D, but can not be stacked. The PieDiagram service provides one property – StartingAngle(Long) which specifies the angle of the first segment of the pie in degrees.

18.3. Chart structure

18.3.1. Title, subtitle and legend

Each type of chart can have a title, subtitle and legend, which have supporting properties provided by the Chart object. The provided properties are:

- HasMainTitle(Boolean) – activates the title.
- Title(Object) – object with detailed information about the chart .
- HasSubTitle(Boolean) – activates the subtitle.
- Subtitle(Object) – object with detailed information about the chart .
- HasLegend(Boolean) – activates the legend.
- Legend(Object) – object with detailed information about the legend.

The com.sun.star.chart.ChartTitle and com.sun.star.chart.ChartLegend services additionally provide properties for determining the size and position of item, together with fill and line characteristics. The ChartTitle also contains the following properties:

- String(String) – text which to be displayed as the title or subtitle.
- TextRotation(Long) – angle of rotation of text in 100ths of a degree.

Additionally, the ChartLegend also provides the following property:

- Alignment(Enum) – position at which the legend appears.

The code below creates a chart and then adds a title and legend to it and formats them:

```
Dim Charts As Object
Dim Chart as Object
Dim Rect As New com.sun.star.awt.Rectangle
Dim RangeAddress(0) As New com.sun.star.table.CellRangeAddress

Rect.X = 8000
Rect.Y = 1000
Rect.Width = 10000
Rect.Height = 7000
RangeAddress(0).Sheet = 0
RangeAddress(0).StartColumn = 0
```

```
RangeAddress(0).StartRow = 0
RangeAddress(0).EndColumn = 2
RangeAddress(0).EndRow = 12

Charts = ThisComponent.Sheets(0).Charts
Charts.addNewByName("MyChart", Rect, RangeAddress(), True, True)
Chart = Charts.getByName("MyChart").EmbeddedObject
Chart.HasMainTitle = True
Chart.Title.String = "Main Title String"
Chart.HasLegend = True
Chart.Legend.Alignment = com.sun.star.chart.ChartLegendPosition.BOTTOM
Chart.Legend.FillStyle = com.sun.star.drawing.FillStyle.SOLID
Chart.Legend.FillColor = RGB(210, 210, 210)
Chart.Legend.CharHeight = 7
```

18.3.2. Background

Each chart type has a background area and the Chart object provides the Area property for formatting it. The com.sun.star.chart.ChartArea service provides properties for lines and fills. For example, the code below will set the background colour to Blue

```
Chart.Area.FillStyle = com.sun.star.drawing.FillStyle.SOLID
Chart.Area.FillColor = RGB(0, 132, 209)
```

18.3.3. Wall and floor

The chart wall is the background behind the coordinate area of the chart object. 3D charts normally have two walls, one behind the plotted data and one to the left-hand or right-hand edge. 3D charts also normally have a floor below the plotted data.

The Diagram object provides Wall and Floor properties for interacting with the wall and floor. These support the com.sun.star.chart.ChartArea service providing the usual fill and line properties.

18.3.4. Axes

OpenOffice.org provides five different axes that can be used in a chart. These are as follows –

- The standard X-axis.
- The standard Y-axis.
- A secondary X-axis, used for scaling where 2 different sets of values are displayed.
- A secondary Y-axis, again used when 2 different sets of values are displayed.
- A Z-axis, used with 3D charts.

The Diagram object provides access to the axes using the following properties –

- HasXAxis(Boolean) – activates the X-axis.
- XAxis(Object) – object with detailed information about the X-axis.
- HasXAxisDescription(Boolean) – activates the labels for the interval marks for the X-axis.
- HasYAxis(Boolean) – activates the Y-axis.
- YAxis(Object) – object with detailed information about the Y-axis.
- HasYAxisDescription(Boolean) – activates the labels for the interval marks for the Y-axis.
- HasZAxis(Boolean) – activates the Z-axis.
- ZAxis(Object) – object with detailed information about the Z-axis.
- HasZAxisDescription(Boolean) – activates the labels for the interval marks for the Z-axis.
- HasSecondaryXAxis(Boolean) – activates the secondary X-axis.
- SecondaryXAxis(Object) – object with detailed information about the secondary X-axis.
- HasSecondaryXAxisDescription(Boolean) – activates the labels for the interval marks for the secondary X-axis.
- HasSecondaryYAxis(Boolean) – activates the secondary Y-axis.
- SecondaryYAxis(Object) – object with detailed information about the secondary Y-axis.
- HasSecondaryYAxisDescription(Boolean) – activates the labels for the interval marks for the secondary Y-axis.

18.3.5. Axes properties

In addition to the properties detailed previously, the Axis object support the com.sun.star.chart.ChartAxis service, which provides a number of additional properties broken down in to specific groups.

Scaling properties –

- Max(Double) – maximum value for axis.
- Min(Double) – minimum value for axis.
- Origin(Double) – point of intersect for crossing axes
- StepMain(Double) – distance between the major interval marks.
- StepHelpCount(Long) – Contains the number of minor intervals within a major interval.
- AutoMax(Boolean) – the maximum value for the axis is calculated automatically when set to true.
- AutoMin(Boolean) – the minimum value for the axis is calculated automatically when set to true.
- AutoOrigin(Boolean) – the origin is determined automatically when set to true.
- AutoStepMain(Boolean) – StepMain is determined automatically when set to true.
- AutoStepHelp(Boolean) – StepHelpCount is determined automatically when set to true.
- Logarithmic(Boolean) – scales the axes in logarithmic manner (rather than linear).
- ReverseDirection(Boolean) – determines if the axis orientation is mathematical or reversed.

Label properties –

- DisplayLabels(Boolean) – activates the text label at the interval marks.
- TextRotation(Long) – angle of rotation of text label in 100ths of a degree.
- ArrangeOrder(enum) – the label may be staggered, thus they are positioned alternately over two lines.
- TextBreak(Boolean) – permits line breaks within the axes labels.
- TextCanOverlap(Boolean) – permits an overlap of the axes labels.
- NumberFormat(Long) – number format to be used with the axes labels.
- LinkNumberFormatToSource(Boolean) – determines whether to use the number format given by the container document, or from the property NumberFormat.

Interval mark properties –

- Marks(Const) – determines the position of the major interval marks.
- HelpMarks(Const) – determines the position of the minor interval marks.

Bar chart properties –

- Overlap(Long) – percentage which specifies the extent to which the bars of different sets of data may overlap.
- GapWidth(long) – percentage which specifies the distance there may be between the different groups of bars of a chart.

18.3.6. Axes Titles

For all axes an additional title can be displayed. The Diagram object provides the following properties to access the axes title:

- HasXAxisTitle(Boolean) – activates title of X-axis
- XAxisTitle(Object) – object with detailed information about title of the X-axis.
- HasYAxisTitle(Boolean) – activates title of Y-axis
- YAxisTitle(Object) – object with detailed information about title of the Y-axis.
- HasZAxisTitle(Boolean) – activates title of Z-axis
- ZAxisTitle(Object) – object with detailed information about title of the Z-axis.
- HasSecondaryXAxisTitle(Boolean) – activates title of the secondary X-axis.
- SecondXAxisTitle(Object) – object with detailed information about title of the secondary X-axis.
- HasSecondaryYAxisTitle(Boolean) – activates title of the secondary Y-axis.
- SecondYAxisTitle(Object) – object with detailed information about title of the secondary Y-axis.

18.3.7. Grids

It is possible to display grids relating to the primary axes, which match to the major and minor intervals. The following properties are provided by the Diagram object to access these grids –

- HasXAxisGrid(Boolean) – activates major grid for X-axis.
- XMainGrid(Object) – object with detailed information about the major grid for X-axis.
- HasXAxisHelpGrid(Boolean) – activates minor grid for X-axis.
- XHelpGrid(Object) – object with detailed information about the minor grid for X-axis.
- HasYAxisGrid(Boolean) – activates major grid for Y-axis.
- YMainGrid(Object) – object with detailed information about the major grid for Y-axis.
- HasYAxisHelpGrid(Boolean) – activates minor grid for Y-axis.
- YHelpGrid(Object) – object with detailed information about the minor grid for Y-axis.
- HasZAxisGrid(Boolean) – activates major grid for Z-axis.
- ZMainGrid(Object) – object with detailed information about the major grid for Z-axis.
- HasZAxisHelpGrid(Boolean) – activates minor grid for Z-axis.
- ZHelpGrid(Object) – object with detailed information about the minor grid for Z-axis.

18.3.8. Axes and grids example

The following code creates a line chart with a white background with a blue grid. The max and min values of the Y-axis are fixed and a title is added to the X-axis –

```
Dim Charts As Object
Dim Chart as Object
Dim Rect As New com.sun.star.awt.Rectangle
Dim RangeAddress(0) As New com.sun.star.table.CellRangeAddress

Charts = ThisComponent.Sheets(0).Charts

Rect.X = 8000
Rect.Y = 1000
Rect.Width = 10000
Rect.Height = 7000
RangeAddress(0).Sheet = 0
RangeAddress(0).StartColumn = 0
RangeAddress(0).StartRow = 0
```

```
RangeAddress(0).EndColumn = 2
RangeAddress(0).EndRow = 12

Charts.addNewByName("MyChart", Rect, RangeAddress(), True, True)
Chart = Charts.getByName("MyChart").embeddedObject
Chart.Diagram = Chart.createInstance("com.sun.star.chart.LineDiagram")
Chart.Diagram.Wall.FillColor = RGB(255, 255, 255)
Chart.Diagram.HasXAxisGrid = True
Chart.Diagram.XMainGrid.LineColor = RGB(0, 0, 255)
Chart.Diagram.HasYAxisGrid = True
Chart.Diagram.YMainGrid.LineColor = RGB(0, 0, 255)
Chart.Diagram.YAxis.Min = 0
Chart.Diagram.YAxis.Max = 100

Chart.Diagram.HasXAxisTitle = True
Chart.Diagram.XAxisTitle.String = "X-axis Title"
```

18.3.9. 3D charts

Most charts in OpenOffice.org can also be displayed with 3D graphics. The following properties are provided for 3D charts by the Diagram object –

- Dim3D(Boolean) – activates 3D display
- Deep(Boolean) – the series will be arranged behind each other in z-direction
- RightAngledAxes(Boolean) – activates a 3D display mode where X- and Y-axes form a right angle within the projection.
- D3DScenePerspective(Enum) – defines whether the 3D objects are to be drawn in perspective or parallel projection.
- Perspective(Long) – Perspective of 3D charts.
- RotationHorizontal(Long) – Horizontal rotation of 3D charts in degrees.
- RotationVertical(Long) – Vertical rotation of 3D charts in degrees.

18.3.10. Stacked charts

Stacked charts are charts that are arranged with several individual values on top of one another to produce a total value. This view shows not only the individual values, but also an overview of all the values. In OpenOffice.org, charts which can be stacked support the com.sun.star.chart.StackableDiagram service, which provides the following properties –

- Stacked(Boolean) – activates the stacked viewing mode.
- Percent(Boolean) – displays percentage distribution rather than absolute values.

19. Databases

19.1. Introduction

OpenOffice.org has a database interface built in, which is called Star Database Connectivity (SDBC).

You can incorporate databases into OpenOffie.org using a data source. The user interface provides an option for creating data sources in the Extras menu, but you can also create them using Basic.

The starting point for interacting with data sources is a database context object, which is created using the createUnoService function to create an instance of the com.sun.star.sdb.DatabaseContext service.

The following example creates a database context and then uses it to display the names of all the data sources available –

```
Dim DatabaseContext As Object
Dim Names
Dim I As Integer

DatabaseContext = createUnoService("com.sun.star.sdb.DatabaseContext")

Names = DatabaseContext.getElementNames()

For I = 0 To UBound(Names())
    MsgBox Names(I)
Next I
```

Individual data sources are based on the com.sun.star.sdb.DataSource service and can be accessed using the getByName method of the DatabaseContext object. Data sources provide a number of properties, which provide information about the data and its access methods. These properties are –

- Name(String) – name of data source
- URL(String) – URL of data source.
- Settings(Array) – array containing PropertyValue-pairs with connection parameters.
- User(String) – user name.
- Password(String) – user password.
- IsPasswordRequired(Boolean) – the password is needed and is interactively requested from user.
- IsReadOnly(Boolean) – permits read-only access to the database

- NumberFormatsSupplier(Object) – object containing the number formats available for the database.
- TableFilter(Array) – list of table names to be displayed.
- TableTypeFilter(Array) – list of table types to be displayed. Values available are TABLE, VIEW and SYSTEM TABLE.
- SuppressVersionColumns(Boolean) – suppresses the display of columns that are used for version administration.

19.2. Queries

A data source can have predefined queries assigned to it, which can be accessed using the QueryDefinitions method of the data source. The following example loops through all the queries and displays their names –

```
Dim DatabaseContext As Object
Dim DataSource As Object
Dim QueryDefinitions As Object
Dim QueryDefinition As Object
Dim I As Integer

DatabaseContext = createUnoService("com.sun.star.sdb.DatabaseContext")
DataSource = DatabaseContext.getByName("Users")
QueryDefinitions = DataSource.getQueryDefinitions()

For I = 0 To QueryDefinitions.Count() - 1
    QueryDefinition = QueryDefinitions(I)
    MsgBox QueryDefinition.Name
Next I
```

In addition to the Name property used above, the QueryDefinitions service provides a Command property that holds the SQL command. The example below creates a query object and assigns it to a data source –

```
Dim DatabaseContext As Object
Dim DataSource As Object
Dim QueryDefinitions As Object
Dim QueryDefinition As Object

DatabaseContext = createUnoService("com.sun.star.sdb.DatabaseContext")
DataSource = DatabaseContext.getByName("Users")
QueryDefinitions = DataSource.getQueryDefinitions()
QueryDefinition = createUnoService("com.sun.star.sdb.QueryDefinition")
QueryDefinition.Command = "SELECT * FROM User"
QueryDefinitions.insertByName("NewQuery", QueryDefinition)
```

19.3. Database access

To access a database, a database connection is required, which permits direct communication with the database. There are various ways of creating database connections. The example below shows how to connect to an existing data source.

```
Dim DatabaseContext As Object
Dim DataSource As Object
Dim Connection As Object
Dim InteractionHandler as Object

DatabaseContext = createUnoService("com.sun.star.sdb.DatabaseContext")
DataSource = DatabaseContext.getByName("Users")

If Not DataSource.IsPasswordRequired Then
    Connection = DataSource.GetConnection("", "")
Else
    InteractionHandler = createUnoService("com.sun.star.sdb.InteractionHandler")
    Connection = DataSource.ConnectWithCompletion(InteractionHandler)
End If
```

19.3.1. Table iteration

Once a database connection has been established, a table can be accessed through a ResultSet object. The following example builds on the previous code and generates a ResultSet using a SELECT query and then loops through each of the returned results, displaying the value of the first column –

```
Statement = Connection.createStatement()
ResultSet = Statement.executeQuery("SELECT ""UserName"" FROM ""User""")

If Not IsNull(ResultSet) Then
    While ResultSet.next
        MsgBox ResultSet.getString(1)
    Wend
End If
```

19.3.2. Type-specific methods for value retrieval

The previous example shows the getString method for retrieving string values. The following additional methods are provided for retrieving values from ResultSets –

- getByte() – supports the SQL data types for numbers, characters and strings.
- getShort() – supports the SQL data types for numbers, characters and strings.
- getInt() – supports the SQL data types for numbers, characters and strings.
- getLong() – supports the SQL data types for numbers, characters and strings.
- getFloat() – supports the SQL data types for numbers, characters and strings.
- getDouble() – supports the SQL data types for numbers, characters and strings.
- getBoolean() – supports the SQL data types for numbers, characters and strings.
- getString() – supports all SQL data types.
- getBytes() – supports the SQL data types for binary values.
- getDate() – supports the SQL data types for numbers, strings, date and time stamp.
- getTime() – supports the SQL data types for numbers, strings, date and time stamp.
- getTimestamp() – supports the SQL data types for numbers, strings, date and time stamp.
- getCharacterStream() – supports the SQL data types for numbers, strings and binary values.
- getUnicodeStream() – supports the SQL data types for numbers, strings and binary values.
- getBinaryStream() – binary values.
- getObject() – supports all SQL data types.

19.3.3. ResultSet variations

The basic ResultSet used in the previous example only provides for navigating forward through the set and does not allow for updating the values. The Statement object that is used to create the ResultSet can specify additional navigation and update options, using the following properties –

- ResultSetConcurrency(const) – specifications as to whether the data can be modified.
- ResultSetType(const) – specifications regarding the navigation of the data.

The values available to ResultSetConcurrency are –

- UPDATABLE – the ResultSet permits values to be modified.
- READ_ONLY – the ResultSet does not permit modifications.

The values available to ResultSetType are –

- FORWARD_ONLY – The ResultSet only permits forward navigation.
- SCROLL_INSENSITIVE – The ResultSet permits any type of navigation, changes to the original data are, however, not noted.
- SCROLL_SENSITIVE – The ResultSet permits any type of navigation, changes to the original data impact on the ResultSet.

19.3.4.   ResultSet navigation

If either of the SCROLL navigation methods are used then there are a number of methods available for navigating through the ResultSet. The key methods are –

- next() – navigate to the next data record.
- previous() – navigate to the previous data record.
- first() – navigate to the first data record.
- last() – navigate to the last data record.
- beforeFirst() – navigate to before the first data record.
- afterLast() – navigate to after the last data record.

There are also a number of test methods to determine the current cursor position –

- isBeforeFirst() – Cursor is before the first data record
- isAfterLast() – Cursor is after the last data record
- isFirst() – Cursor is at the first data record
- isLast() – Cursor is at the last data record

19.3.5.   Modifying data records

If a ResultSet has been created with the concurrency set to UPDATEABLE, then its content can be modified.

The ResultSet object provides corresponding update methods to the get methods described previously. For example, updateString updates a string value.

Once a value has been modified, it must be transferred to the database using the updateRow() method. This must be done before any navigation takes place.

If an error is made during the modification then it can be undone using the cancelRowUpdates() method, before updateRow() is called.

20. Dialogs

20.1. Introduction

OpenOffice.org dialogs are windows that can contain text fields, radio buttons, drop-down lists and other control elements.

Dialogs can be created in the IDE by using the Macro Organizer and selecting the Dialogs tab. From here new dialogs can be created and existing ones edited.

This will open up the dialog for editing, and allow you to add the various elements to it.

20.2. Accessing dialogs

20.2.1. Displaying dialogs

Dialogs can be programmatically accessed, as can be seen in the following code –

```
Dim Dlg As Object

DialogLibraries.LoadLibrary("Standard")
Dlg = CreateUnoDialog(DialogLibraries.Standard.DlgDef)
Dlg.Execute()
Dlg.dispose()
```

First, you have to make sure that the library that the dialog uses is loaded. This is done using the LoadLibrary method. The dialog can then be created using the CreateUnoDialog method and then displayed using the Execute method.

Dialogs such as this are described as being modal – while they are displayed, no further program action is permitted. Once the dialog is exited, its resources are released using the dispose method.

20.2.2. Closing dialogs

Closing with OK or Cancel

Where a dialog contains an OK or Cancel button, the dialog is automatically closed when one of these buttons is pressed. If the OK button is clicked then the **Execute** method will return a 1, otherwise a 0 is returned. The following code determines whether OK or Cancel was pressed –

```
Dim Dlg As Object

DialogLibraries.LoadLibrary("Standard")
Dlg = CreateUnoDialog(DialogLibraries.Standard.MyDialog)
Select Case Dlg.Execute()
Case 1
    MsgBox "Ok pressed"
Case 0
    MsgBox "Cancel pressed"
End Select
```

Closing with the close button in the title bar

You can close a dialog by clicking the close button on the title bar of the dialog window. The Execute method of the dialog returns the value 0, which is the same as when Cancel is clicked.

Closing with an explicit program call

From a routine called by an event of a control, e.g. push of a normal button, you can also close an open dialog window with the endExecute method –

```
Dlg.endExecute()
```

Calling the endExecute method will return a 0, the same as clicking on the Cancel button. A better option is to use the endDialog method, as this takes an argument which will be the return value.

20.2.3. Access to control elements

It is also possible to access the many control elements contained within a dialog. This is achieved using the getControl method that obtains an element by name. For example, the below code gets the object for the MyButton control element and then sets its label to "New Label".

```
Dim Ctl As Object

Ctl = Dlg.getControl("MyButton")
Ctl.Label = "New Label"
```

20.3. Control element properties

Each element within a dialog has properties that can be accessed programmatically. The Model object provides for the access to the properties of dialogs and elements.

20.3.1. Name and title

Each control element has a name, which can be used to access it. This name is set using the Name property –

- Model.Name(String) – control element name.

It is also possible to specify the title that appears in the title bar of a dialog, using the Title property –

- Model.Title(String) – dialog title.

20.3.2. Size and position

You can access the size and position of a control element using the following properties –

- Model.Height(long) – height of control element.
- Model.Width(long) – width of control element.
- Model.PositionX(long) – X-position of control element, measured from the left inner edge of the dialog.
- Model.PositionY(long) – Y-position of control element, measured from top inner edge of the dialog.

20.3.3. Tab sequence

It is possible to navigate through the elements of a dialog by using the Tab key. The Model object makes a number of properties available for dealing with this –

- Model.Enabled(Boolean) – activates the control element.
- Model.Tabstop(Boolean) – allows the control element to be reached through the Tab key.
- Model.TabIndex(Long) – position of control element in the order of activation.

20.3.4. Multi-page dialogs

Dialogs in OpenOffice.org can be made up of more than one page. The Step property of a dialog defines which page is currently being displayed. The corresponding Step property of an element determines which page the element should be displayed on.

The Step value of 0 is a special case. On a dialog, if this value is set then all elements will be displayed regardless of their Step value. On an element, a Step value of 0 indicates that the element should be displayed on all pages.

The code below shows how a "Next" button that moves from one page to another of a two page dialog could be programmed. The Dlg variable is a global variable that refers to the dialog.

```
Sub cmdNext_Pressed
    Dim cmdNext As Object

    cmdNext = Dlg.getControl("cmdNext")
    cmdNext.Model.Enabled = False
    Dlg.Model.Step = Dlg.Model.Step + 1
End Sub
```

20.4. Dialog events

OpenOffice.org dialogs operate in an event-oriented programming model, where you can assign event handlers to control elements. An event handler will trigger a predefined procedure when a particular event occurs. There are four main groups of event types –

- **Mouse control**: Events that correspond to mouse actions (for example, simple mouse movements or a click on a particular screen location).
- **Keyboard control**: Events that are triggered by keyboard strokes.
- **Focus modification**: Events that OpenOffice.org performs when control elements are activated or deactivated.
- **Control element-specific events**: Events that only occur in relation to certain control elements.

Events can be assigned by right clicking on a control element within the IDE ansd selecting the properties option. This will display the properties dialog and you should select the Events tab –

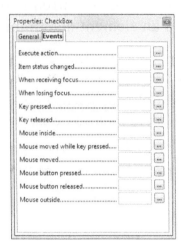

You can then press on the … after the event you wish to assign a procedure to. This will bring up the "Assign action" dialog –

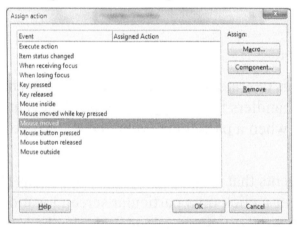

You can then click on the "Macro…" button and select the macro you wish to assign.

20.4.1. Mouse events

The following mouse related events are recognised by OpenOffice.org –

- Mouse moved – user moves mouse.
- Mouse moved while key pressed – user drags mouse while holding down a key.
- Mouse button pressed – user presses a mouse button.
- Mouse button released – user releases a mouse button.
- Mouse outside – user moves mouse outside of the current window.

The associated event objects that are generated are defined in the com.sun.star.awt.MouseEvent structure, which provides the following properties –

- Buttons(short) – button pressed (constants defined by com.sun.star.awt.MouseButton).
- X(long) – X-coordinate of mouse, measured in pixels from the top left corner of the control element.
- Y(long) – Y-coordinate of mouse, measured in pixels from the top left corner of the control element.
- ClickCount(long) – number of clicks associated with the mouse event.

The constants defined for the mouse buttons in com.sun.star.awt.MouseButton are –

- LEFT – left mouse button
- RIGHT – right mouse button
- MIDDLE – middle mouse button

The following procedure could be attached to a mouse button press event and will report which button was pressed and the position of the mouse at the time of the event –

```
Sub MouseUp(Event As Object)
    Dim Msg As String
    Msg = "Keys: "
    If Event.Buttons AND com.sun.star.awt.MouseButton.LEFT Then
        Msg = Msg & "LEFT "
    End If
    If Event.Buttons AND com.sun.star.awt.MouseButton.RIGHT Then
        Msg = Msg & "RIGHT "
    End If
    If Event.Buttons AND com.sun.star.awt.MouseButton.MIDDLE Then
        Msg = Msg & "MIDDLE "
    End If
    Msg = Msg & Chr(13) & "Position: "
    Msg = Msg & Event.X & "/" & Event.Y
    MsgBox Msg
End Sub
```

20.4.2. Keyboard events

The following keyboard related events are supported by OpenOffice.org –

- Key pressed – user presses a key.
- Key released – user releases a key

The event that is created provides the following properties relating to the event –

- KeyCode(short) – code of the pressed key.
- KeyChar(String) – character that is entered.

20.4.3. Focus events

Focus events are triggered when an element gains or loses focus. The following focus related events are available to OpenOffice.org –

- When receiving focus – element receives focus.
- When losing focus – element loses focus.

The Event object that is created provides the following properties –

- FocusFlags(short) – cause of focus change (value in accordance with com.sun.star.awt.FocusChangeReason)
- NextFocus(Object) – object that receives focus (only for the When losing focus event)
- Temporary(Boolean) – the focus is temporarily lost

20.4.4. Element specific events

The previously detailed events are supported by all control elements. Additionally, there are some control element-specific events that are only supported by certain control elements. Some of these are –

- When Item Changed – the value of a control element changes.
- Item Status Changed – the status of a control element changes.
- Text modified – the text of a control element changes.
- When initiating – an action that can be performed when the control element is triggered.

21. Forms

The structure of OpenOffice.org forms is similar to dialogs, but with some key differences –

- Dialogs appear in the form of one single dialog window, which is displayed over the document, whereas Forms are displayed directly in the document.
- A dialog editor is provided for creating dialogs in the OpenOffice.org Basic development environment. Forms, on the other hand, are created using the Form Controls and the Form Design Toolbar directly within the document.
- Whereas the dialog functions are available in all OpenOffice.org documents, the full scope of the form functions are only available in text and spreadsheets.
- The control elements of a form can be linked with an external database table. This function is not available in dialogs.

21.1. Working with form objects

Within OpenOffice.org, Forms are accessed using drawing objects. The method of accessing the forms differs between Write and Calc documents. To access a form in Write, the following code can be used to get the form with the index number 0 –

```
Dim DrawPage As Object
Dim Form As Object

DrawPage = ThisComponent.DrawPage
Form = DrawPage.Forms.GetByIndex(0)
```

When accessing a form in Calc, an intermediate stage is required because the drawing objects are held at Sheet rather than Document level –

```
Dim Sheet As Object
Dim DrawPage As Object
Dim Form As Object

Sheet = ThisComponent.Sheets.GetByIndex(0)
DrawPage = Sheet.DrawPage
Form = DrawPage.Forms.GetByIndex(0)
```

21.2. Control element aspects

The control elements of a form have three distinct aspects –

- The **Model** of the control element is the key object for the OpenOffice.org Basic-programmer when working with control element forms.
- The counterpart to this is the **View** of the control element, which administers the display information.
- Since control element forms within the documents are administered like a special drawing element, there is also a **Shape** object which reflects the drawing element-specific properties of the control element.

21.2.1. The model aspect

The model of a control element is accessed through the GetByName method of the Form object –

```
Dim Form As Object
Dim Ctl As Object

Form = ThisComponent.DrawPage.Forms.GetByIndex(0)
Ctl = Form.getByName("MyListBox")
```

An additional method hasByName can be used to check whether a Form contains a named control element.

21.2.2. The view aspect

To access the view of a control element, you must first access the associated model. You will also need the documents controller, as can be seen below –

```
Dim DocCrl As Object
Dim Form As Object
Dim Ctl As Object
Dim CtlView As Object

DocCrl = ThisComponent.getCurrentController()
Form = ThisComponent.DrawPage.Forms.GetByIndex(0)
Ctl = Form.getByName("MyListBox")
CtlView = DocCrl.GetControl(Ctl)
```

21.2.3. The shape aspect

To access the shape aspect of a control element, it is necessary to loop through all the drawing elements to find the required one –

```
Dim Shape As Object
Dim I As Integer

For I = 0 to ThisComponent.DrawPage.Count - 1
    Shape = ThisComponent.DrawPage(I)
    If HasUnoInterfaces(Shape, "com.sun.star.drawing.XControlShape") Then
        If Shape.Control.Name = "MyListBox" Then
            Exit Function
        End If
    End If
Next
```

21.2.4. Control element size and position

Once you have access to the Shape aspect of a control element, it is possible to determine its size and position. The Shape object provides Size and Position properties for this purpose.

21.3. Control element types

Forms provide a number of different control elements. These range from simple text fields through list and combo boxes to various buttons. This section describes the elements that are available.

21.3.1. Buttons

The button form element provides the following properties –

- BackgroundColor (long) – background colour.
- DefaultButton (Boolean) – the button serves as a default value. In this case, it also responds to the entry button if it has no focus.
- Enabled (Boolean) – the control element can be activated.
- Tabstop (Boolean) – the control element can be reached through the tab button.
- TabIndex (Long) – position of control element in activation sequence.
- FontName (String) – name of font type.
- FontHeight (Single) – height of character in points (pt).
- Tag (String) – string containing additional information, which can be saved in the button for program-controlled access.
- TargetURL (String) – target URL for buttons of the URL type.
- TargetFrame (String) – name of window (or frame) in which TargetURL is to be opened when activating the button (for buttons of the URL type).
- Label (String) – button label.
- TextColor (Long) – text colour of control element.
- HelpText (String) – automatically displayed help text which is displayed if the mouse cursor is above the control element.
- HelpURL (String) – URL of online help for the corresponding control element.
- ButtonType (Enum) – action that is linked with the button.
- State (Short) – in toggle button, 1 = pushed, 0 = normal.

21.3.2. Option buttons

Option button elements provide the following properties –

- Enabled (Boolean) – the control element can be activated.
- Tabstop (Boolean) – the control element can be reached through the tab key.
- TabIndex (Long) – position of control element in the activation sequence.
- FontName (String) – name of font type.
- FontHeight (Single) – height of character in points (pt).
- Tag (String) – string containing additional information, which can be saved in the button for program-controlled access.
- Label (String) – inscription of button.
- Printable (Boolean) – the control element can be printed.
- State (Short) – if 1, the option is activated, otherwise it is deactivated.
- RefValue (String) – string for saving additional information.
- TextColor (Long) – text colour of control element.
- HelpText (String) – automatically displayed help text, which is displayed if the mouse cursor is above the control element.
- HelpURL (String) – URL of online help for the corresponding control element.

21.3.3. Checkboxes

Checkbox elements provide the following properties –

- Enabled (Boolean) – the control element can be activated.
- Tabstop (Boolean) – the control element can be reached through the tab key.
- TabIndex (Long) – position of control element in the activation sequence.
- FontName (String) – name of font type.
- FontHeight (Single) – height of character in points (pt).
- Tag (String) – string containing additional information, which can be saved in the button for program-controlled access.
- Label (String) – button label.
- Printable (Boolean) – the control element can be printed.
- State (Short) – if 1, the option is activated, otherwise it is deactivated.
- RefValue (String) – string for saving additional information.
- TextColor (Long) – text colour of control element.
- HelpText (String) – automatically displayed help text, which is displayed if the mouse cursor is above the control element.
- HelpURL (String) – URL of online help for the corresponding control element.

21.3.4. Text fields

Text field elements provide the following properties –

- Align (short) – orientation of text (0: left-aligned, 1: centered, 2: right-aligned).
- BackgroundColor (long) – background colour of control element.
- Border (short) – type of border (0: no border, 1: 3D border, 2: simple border).
- EchoChar (String) – echo character for password field.
- FontName (String) – name of font type.
- FontHeight (Single) – height of character in points (pt).
- HardLineBreaks (Boolean) – the automatic line breaks are permanently inserted in the text of the control element.
- HScroll (Boolean) – the text has a horizontal scrollbar.
- MaxTextLen (Short) – maximum length of text; if 0 is specified, there are no limits.
- MultiLine (Boolean) – permits multi-line entries.
- Printable (Boolean) – the control element can be printed.
- ReadOnly (Boolean) – the content of the control element is read-only.
- Enabled (Boolean) – the control element can be activated.
- Tabstop (Boolean) – the control element can be reached through the tab key.
- TabIndex (Long) – position of the control element in the activation sequence.
- FontName (String) – name of font type.
- FontHeight (Single) – height of character in points (pt).
- Text (String) – text of control element.
- TextColor (Long) – text colour of control element.
- VScroll (Boolean) – the text has a vertical scrollbar.
- HelpText (String) – automatically displayed help text, which is displayed if the mouse cursor is above the control element.
- HelpURL (String) – URL of online help for the corresponding control element.

21.3.5. List Boxes

List box elements provide the following properties –

- BackgroundColor (long) – background color of control element.
- Border (short) – type of border (0: no border, 1: 3D frame, 2: simple frame).
- FontDescriptor (struct) – structure with details of font to be used.
- LineCount (Short) – number of lines of control element.
- MultiSelection (Boolean) – permits multiple selection of entries.
- SelectedItems (Array of Strings) – list of highlighted entries.
- StringItemList (Array of Strings) – list of all entries.
- ValueItemList (Array of Variant) – list containing additional information for each entry.
- Printable (Boolean) – the control element can be printed.
- ReadOnly (Boolean) – the content of the control element is read-only.
- Enabled (Boolean) – the control element can be activated.
- Tabstop (Boolean) – the control element can be reached through the tab key.
- TabIndex (Long) – position of control element in the activation sequence.
- FontName (String) – name of font type.
- FontHeight (Single) – height of character in points (pt).
- Tag (String) – string containing additional information which can be saved in the button for program-controlled access.
- TextColor (Long) – text color of control element.
- HelpText (String) – automatically displayed help text, which is displayed if the mouse cursor is above the control element.
- HelpURL (String) – URL of online help for the corresponding control element.

Additionally, through the view object of the element, the following properties are available –

- addItem (Item, Pos) – inserts the string specified in the Item at the Pos position in the list.
- addItems (ItemArray, Pos) – inserts the entries listed in the string's ItemArray data field in the list at the Pos position.
- removeItems (Pos, Count) – removes Count entries as of the Pos position.
- selectItem (Item, SelectMode) – activates or deactivates the highlighting for the element specified in the string Item depending on the SelectMode variable.
- makeVisible (Pos) – scrolls through the list field so that the entry specified by Pos is visible.

Appendix I

The following options are available for the Properties argument of the loadComponentFromURL function:

Option	Description
AsTemplate	Takes a Boolean value, if True then a new untitled document is loaded based on the template specified in the URL. If False then the template is loaded for editing.
CharacterSet	Defines which set of characters a document is based on.
FilterName	Specifies a special filter to be used, for example for loading .csv files.
FilterData	Additional options data for the filter.
Hidden	Takes a Boolean value, if True then the document is loaded in invisible mode.
JumpMark	Once the document has been opened, jump to the position defined by the value.
MacroExecutionMode	Indicates whether document macros can be executed.
Password	Passes the password required for a protected file.
ReadOnly	Takes a Boolean value, if True then the document is opened read-only.
UpdateDocMode	Indicates how/if links will be updated.

Appendix II

The following options are available for the Properties argument of the storeAsURL function:

Option	Description
CharacterSet	Defines which set of characters a document is based on.
FilterName	Specifies a special filter to be used, for example for loading .csv files.
FilterData	Additional options data for the filter.
Overwrite	Boolean value, True indicates that an existing file should be overwritten.
Password	Passes the password required for a protected file.
Unpacked	Boolean value, True indicates that the file should be stored uncompressed.

Appendix III

The following options are available for the Properties argument of the Print function:

Option	Description
CopyCount	Specifies the number of copies to be printed.
FileName	Prints the document to a file.
Collate	Boolean value, True indicates that pages should be collated.
Sort	Sorts the pages when printing more than 1 copy.
Pages	String specifying the pages to be printed.
Wait	Boolean value, True indicates that the method will not return until the job is fully passed to the printer.

The following options are available for the Printer property:

Option	Description
Name	Specifies the name of the printer.
PaperOrientation	Specifies the orientation of the paper. Accepts the values com.sun.star.view.PaperOrientation.PORTRAIT and com.sun.star.view.PaperOrientation.LANDSCAPE for portrait and landscape respectively.
PaperFormat	Specifies the format of the paper, such as A4 or Legal. Accepts values such as com.sun.star.view.PaperFormat.A4.
PaperSize	Specifies the size of the paper in hundredths of a mm.

Appendix IV

The following methods are available using a TextCursor to navigate through a document:

Method	Description
goLeft(Count, Highlight)	Move the cursor Count characters to the left.
goRight(Count, Highlight)	Move the cursor Count characters to the right.
gotoStart(Highlight)	Move the cursor to the start of the text document.
gotoEnd(Highlight)	Move the cursor to the end of the text document.
gotoRange(TextRange, Highlight)	Move the cursor to the specified TextRange object.
gotoStartOfWord(Highlight)	Move to the start of the current word.
gotoEndOfWord(Highlight)	Move to the end of the current word.
gotoNextWord(Highlight)	Move to the start of the next word.
gotoPreviousWord(Highlight)	Move to the start of the previous word.
isStartOfWord()	Returns True if the TextCursor is at the start of a word.
isEndOfWord()	Returns True if the TextCursor is at the end of a word.
gotoStartOfSentence(Highlight)	Move to the start of the current sentence.
gotoEndOfSentence(Highlight)	Move to the end of the current sentence.
gotoNextSentence(Highlight)	Move to the start of the next sentence.
gotoPreviousSentence(Highlight)	Move to the start of the previous sentence.
isStartOfSentence()	Returns True if the TextCursor is at the start of a sentence.
isEndOfSentence()	Returns True if the TextCursor is at the end of a sentence.
gotoStartOfParagraph(Highlight)	Move to the start of the current paragraph.
gotoEndOfParagraph(Highlight)	Move to the end of the current paragraph.
gotoNextParagraph(Highlight)	Move to the start of the next paragraph.
gotoPreviousParagraph(Highlight)	Move to the start of the previous paragraph.

In all the above methods, the Highlight argument is a Boolean which indicates whether the text moved over is highlighted or not. The goto methods also all return a Boolean value indicating whether the action was successful or not.

CPSIA information can be obtained at www.ICGtesting.com
Printed in the USA
LVOW02s2228130114

369235LV00006B/833/P